CHRISTMAS
CRAFTS

CHRISTMAS CRAFTS

∴∾

Over 50 festive
ideas for every
room in the home

∾∴∾

MYRA DAVIDSON

∾∴∾

CASSELL

A CASSELL BOOK
First published 1994
by Cassell
Villiers House
41/47 Strand
London
WC2N 5JE

Copyright © 1994 Myra Davidson
Design by Bet Ayer
Photography by Paul Bricknell
Illustrations by Peter Bull

Distributed in the United States
by Sterling Publishing Co., Inc.
387 Park Avenue South, New York, New York 10016-8810

Distributed in Australia
by Capricorn Link (Australia) Pty Ltd
2/13 Carrington Road, Castle Hill, NSW 2154

British Library Cataloguing-in-Publication Data
A catalogue record for this book is available from the British Library

ISBN 0-304-34337-4
Typeset by Litho Link Ltd., Welshpool, Powys, Wales
Printed and bound in Italy by New Interlitho SpA

To my seasonal workshop students,
whose enthusiasm gives continual inspiration.

AUTHOR'S ACKNOWLEDGEMENTS

My grateful thanks to Barbara Carpenter and Mary Straka for their much appreciated practical help with typing and reading the text, also for their extremely hard work in designing and making many of the beautiful craft items in the book. My thanks to Paul Hooper for drawing the templates for the patchwork.

I also thank the following suppliers:
The Body Shop International for toiletries; Ebor Craft Fabrics for their very generous supply of material; Newey Goodman Ltd for sewing accessories; C.M. Offray and Son Ltd for ribbons; Perivale-Gutermann Ltd for Sew-all Threads; Pownall Carpets of Manchester for the living room carpet; Rufflette Ltd for curtain tapes; Selectus Ltd for Touch-and-Close fasteners; Vilene Retail for interfacing.

American readers may find it helpful to know the following terms used in the UK:

UK term	US term
cocktail stick	toothpick
craft knife	X-acto knife
drawing-pin	thumbtack
florist's foam	Styrofoam
muslin	cheesecloth
tack	baste
wadding	batting

Imperial measurements are given as well as the metric conversions. Metric conversions are quoted in centimetres, but items such as ribbon and bias binding are quoted in millimetres, as this is how you would buy them in the shop.

∽ CONTENTS ∾

❧ INTRODUCTION ❧

Christmas . . . a time for celebration and family gatherings . . . a time to exchange greeting cards and visit friends. Knowing what pleasure it gives to make decorations, inspired me to write this Christmas Crafts project book based on the one-day workshops that I have been running for several years, assisted by Barbara Carpenter and Mary Straka. We specialize in different aspects of crafts, thus providing a variety of items that require a range of skills of varying levels.

There are lots of ideas in the book on preparing for the festive season to give a touch of Christmas throughout the home. I hope that, with the help of your family and friends, you will enjoy collecting all the components, and making your choice of projects.

· I ·
FRONT DOOR, HALL & STAIRWAY

It is said that first impressions count a lot; they can also kindle great expectations of what lies ahead. When a traditional Christmas wreath hangs on the front door, it can be the beginning of a magical journey that continues through the home. Some say that Christmas is for children, but are not most adults still children at heart?

·

When the front door is opened, a patchwork tree adorning a wall, and a festoon of greenery are revealed. An unusual garland is attached with colourful hitches to the stairway. A small round table has a floor-length cloth with a swagged overlay, which is complemented by a toning table decoration.

❧ DOOR WREATH ❧

The traditional seasonal welcome to the home —
a circle of vine bound with pine, fruits and berries
and trimmed with fabric in the colours chosen for
the entrance hall decorations.

MATERIALS

- Natural vine ring
- Brass curtain ring: 1 ¼ in (32 mm) diameter
- Binding wire
- Securing tape
- Small piece dry florist's foam
- Fabric stiffener
- Pieces of fabric as used in the hall: 40 x 7 in (101.5 x 18 cm) and 45 x 4½ in (114 x 11.5 cm)
- Glue gun
- Pine and spruce branches and sprigs, natural or artificial
- Pine and spruce cones, sprayed gold
- Natural jacaranda pods
- Seasonal fruits and berries, fresh, dried or artificial
- Dried poppyseed heads, sprayed gold
- Canary grass, coloured to tone

1 Choose a point on the vine wreath for the top and attach a brass curtain ring very firmly with wire.

2 Tape the dry florist's foam to the opposite side, which will now become the base of the wreath.

3 Work the fabric stiffener into the wider piece of fabric. Fold lengthways, raw edges to the centre, and hang to dry until slightly damp. Fold into a bow, leaving tails of about 10 in (25.5 cm) and 14 in (35.5 cm). Twist a length of wire round the centre of the bow, pulling the fabric together. Leave to dry.

4 Fold the narrower piece of fabric lengthways, with the right sides together. Pin and machine stitch with a ¼ in (6 mm) seam, removing the pins as you machine. Turn right sides out, roll the seam between fingers and thumbs, tack as you proceed and press, using a damp piece of muslin and a medium-hot iron.

5 Bind this strip around the upper half of the wreath, securing the ends at the back with glue.

6 Lay a framework of short pine and spruce branches along the vine, starting from the foam block and working up each side as far as the fabric binding, securing with wire or hot glue.

7 Wire the spruce cones and attach the largest at the base of the wreath and the smaller ones to the sides. Remember that the foam block will be the focal point and hence most material must be concentrated in this area.

8 Glue the jacaranda pods and some of the fruit among the greenery, adding more where necessary.

9 Insert the prepared fabric bow into the foam block and use short pieces of pine and spruce to fill in around it. Make sure the tails hang down neatly and cut the ends at a slant.

10 Insert a central piece of fruit, the poppyseed heads, the wired pine cones and the remaining fruit and berries, placing them among the fabric loops and generally pointing outwards from the bow.

11 Insert canary grass to soften the outline and add spots of colour.

❧ HANGING PATCHWORK TREE ❧

A little 'tree' of small fabric triangles, which can be made by hand or machine sewing.

MATERIALS

- ⌁ Fabric: offcuts of Christmas fabric from other projects
- ⌁ Thread
- ⌁ Polyester stuffing
- ⌁ Ribbon: 1/8 in (3 mm) wide, 14 in (35.5 cm)
- ⌁ Trimmings such as sequins, small bells and ribbon bows (optional)

1 Trace the template, opposite, and cut out in card. Additional information on tracing templates is given on page 116.

2 Cut out 28 pairs of triangles, having decided on the colour formation.

3 Stitch each pair of triangles, using the 1/4 in (6 mm) seam allowance, by machine or by hand on two sides. Trim the point of the seam and turn right side out.

4 Stuff the triangles. Turn in the seam allowance on the third edge and slip-stitch to close.

5 Following Fig. A, join 25 of the triangles at the points only, to form a large triangle.

6 The three remaining triangles form the 'tub' for the tree. Stitch them to the centre of the bottom row (Fig. B).

7 Stitch a loop of ribbon to the back of the top triangle for hanging and add trimmings.

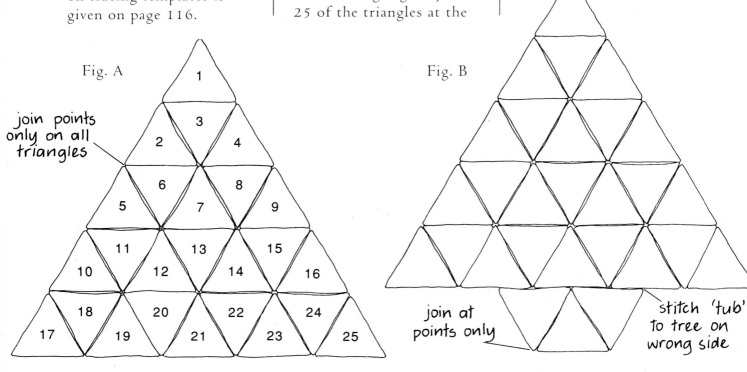

Fig. A

join points only on all triangles

1
2 3 4
5 6 7 8 9
10 11 12 13 14 15 16
17 18 19 20 21 22 23 24 25

Fig. B

join at points only

stitch 'tub' to tree on wrong side

template
(actual size)

❧ FESTOON ❧

A festoon of seasonal fruits and foliage to frame a doorway or decorate a plain wall, linked in colour and fabric with the other hall decorations.

MATERIALS

- Binding wire
- 2 brass curtain rings: 1¼ in (32 mm) diameter
- Curved cane base
- 4 large spruce cones, sprayed gold
- 4 pine cones, sprayed gold
- Assorted short stems of pine, spruce, mistletoe, holly, juniper, cedar or similar
- Glue gun
- 6 jacaranda pods
- 3 pomegranates or silk apples
- 4 stub wires
- Antique white double satin ribbon: 1½ in (39 mm) wide, 2¼ yds (2.10 m)
- Scarlet organza sheer ribbon: 1½ in (39 mm) wide, 4½ yds (4.15 m)
- 4 pieces of fabric to match hall: 4 x 9 in (10 x 23 cm)
- Walnuts, hazels or pecans
- 2 strips of patterned fabric and 2 strips of plain fabric, each measuring about 31 x 5 in (79 x 12.5 cm), for the tails (the lowest point should be approximately level with the lowest item on the festoon)

1 Firmly wire a curtain ring to each end of the curved cane base.

2 Wire the spruce and pine cones, page 115.

3 Attach the two largest spruce cones to the lowest central point of the cane arc and one to each end.

4 Starting from the central point and working up each curved side, insert short stems of greenery into the cane mesh, pointing them toward the ringed ends and securing them with hot glue.

5 Glue the jacaranda pods in groups on either side of the centre, interspersing them with the wired pine cones.

6 Add the fruit centrally and secure with glue.

7 Make four ribbon roses on stub wires, page 115, using the antique white satin ribbon overlaid on both sides with the sheer scarlet ribbon, and insert them into the arrangement diagonally across the centre. Secure the stems to the cane with hot glue.

8 Make four wired loops from the four small pieces of fabric by pressing a ¼ in (6 mm) turning to the wrong side on the longer edges of each piece of fabric. Fold the fabric in half right sides out and unfolded edges together (Fig. A). Gather these raw edges together and bind with wire, thus forming four fabric loops. Insert the loops among the greenery around the fruit, securing them with hot glue.

9 Add nuts to fill any spaces, ensuring that the two sides of the festoon are well-balanced.

TO MAKE THE TAILS
1 Cut each corner of the patterned and plain strips on the bias as shown (Fig. B).

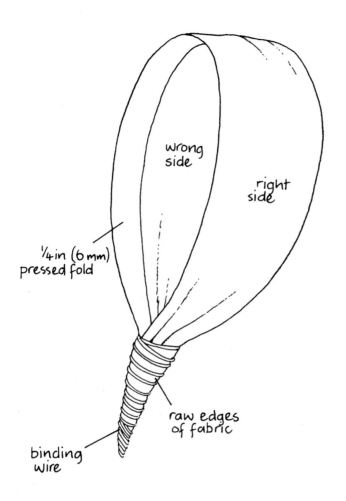

wrong side

right side

¼ in (6 mm) pressed fold

raw edges of fabric

binding wire

Fig. A

cut away shaded areas

Fig. B

2 Stitch a plain strip to a patterned one, right sides together with ½ in (1.3 cm) seam, leaving a gap of 4 in (10 cm) on the longest edge.

3 Trim the seams and corners, and turn right sides out. Turn in the raw edges of the gap and slip-stitch closed.

4 Roll the seam between fingers and thumbs, tack as you proceed and press with a damp piece of muslin and a medium-hot iron.

TO COMPLETE THE FESTOON

1 Fold the tails through the end loops of the cane arc, with the angle of the top tail pointing towards the festoon centre.

2 Wire and glue a berried sprig of holly to each end of the festoon, over the base of the spruce cones, ensuring that the fabric tails hang free for adjustment.

~ ROUND CLOTH WITH ~ SWAGGED OVERLAY

A small round table in the hall is the perfect setting for a plain floor-length cloth, with a swagged overlay made from a patterned fabric. The quantities given are for a table with a 19 in (48.5 cm) diameter and a 24 in (61 cm) drop.

ROUND CLOTH

> ### MATERIALS
>
> ~ Plain fabric: 45 in (114 cm) wide, 4½ yds (4.15 m)
> ~ Thread
> ~ Jumbo cord: 1 in (25 mm) circumference, 6 yds (5.50 m)

1 Make a quarter pattern, using a 33 in (84 cm) square of paper, drawing an arc as shown (Fig. A) and cutting out. Additional instructions for making patterns are given on page 117.

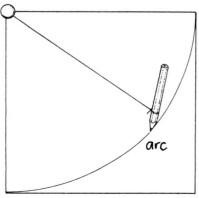

Fig. A

2 Straighten the cut edge of the fabric and cut a length of fabric 67 in (170 cm) long for the full-width central panel of the cloth. Cut two strips 67 in (170 cm) long and 12½ (32 cm) wide.

3 Machine the strips to the sides of the full-width panel with ⅝ in (1.5 cm) seams, and press open.

4 Fold the square of fabric in four and pin to secure the layers. Pin the pattern in position and cut carefully through all layers.

5 Prepare the piping, page 113.

6 Check the cloth on the table to make sure it clears the floor by ½ in (1.3 cm).

7 Pin and tack the piping to the bottom of the cloth, starting 2 in (5 cm) from the end of the piping and leaving an overlap of 2 in (5 cm) at the other end.

8 Machine the piping into place with a zipper foot in position, starting and finishing 2 in (5 cm) from the beginning and end of the piping.

9 Cut the piping straight across on the first end. Turn back the bias strip at the other end and cut the surplus cord off, making sure that the cord ends will butt together. Turn under the bias strip and allow this to cover the raw edge of the first end. Complete machining the piping into place (Fig. B).

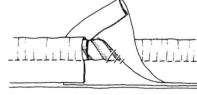

bias strip turned under to cover the first end

Fig. B

10 Remove the tacking, trim the seam to ¼ in (6 mm) and zigzag all raw edges together to neaten. Press the seam upwards.

SWAGGED OVERLAY

MATERIALS

- Patterned fabric: 45 in (114 cm) wide, 1¼ yds (1.15 m)
- Thread to blend with the patterned fabric
- Narrow, lightweight curtain tape: 1½ yds (1.40 m)
- Gold lamé ribbon: 1½ in (39 mm) wide, 3¼ yds (3 m)

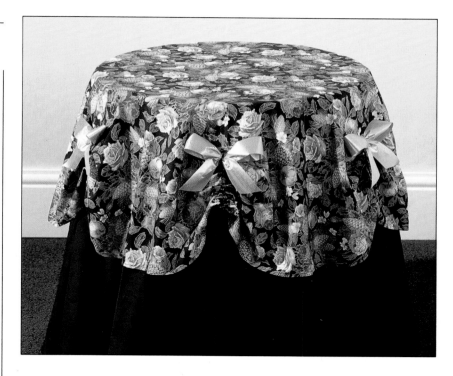

1 Make a quarter pattern, using a 22 in (56 cm) square of paper, drawing an arc as shown (Fig. A, opposite) and cutting out.

2 Fold the fabric in four, ensuring the folds are on the straight and crosswise grains, see page 110. Pin to secure the layers.

3 Pin the pattern in position and cut carefully through all the layers.

4 Machine stitch ½ in (1.3 cm) from the raw edge and using this stitching line as a guide, turn and press to the wrong side.

5 Turn the raw edge to the pressed fold line, tacking as you work round the cloth. Press and then machine stitch. Press again to give a professional finish.

6 Fold the cloth in half and then into three, concertina fashion, and press the folds 8 in (20 cm) up from the hem. This will give the placement lines for the curtain tape.

7 Divide the curtain tape into six equal lengths. Prepare them by pulling the gathering cords at one end of the tape to the wrong side and knotting firmly, turn under ½ in (1.3 cm) and machine across. At the other end pull the gathering cords to the right side, ready to pull up for ruching later,

turn under ½ in (1.3 cm) and machine across, taking care to avoid catching the cords in the stitching.

8 Stitch the pieces of tape to the wrong side of the cloth along the placement lines, with the knotted cords and neatened end positioned just above the hem. Machine both sides of the tape working in the same direction, and across each end.

9 Pull up the gathering cords to obtain the desired depth of the overlay.

10 Using 19 in (48.5 cm) lengths of ribbon, make six bows, page 114, and stitch one at the top of each gathering.

∴ TABLE CENTRE ∾

A classic table arrangement, interpreting three-dimensionally the pattern of the cloth, and linked in style and colour with the welcoming wreath and the festoon.

MATERIALS

- Gold wire-edged ribbon: 2¾ in (68 mm), ⅞ yd (80 cm)
- Round straw or cork mat: about 4 in (10 cm) diameter
- Glue gun
- Block of dry florist's foam
- Florist's plastic anchor
- Florist's plasticine fix
- Adhesive tape
- 4 cocktail sticks
- Gold candle: 10 in (25.5 cm)
- Binding wire
- Forest green velvet craft ribbon: 1½ in (39 mm) wide, 1⅞ yds (1.75 m)
- Forest green wire-edged taffeta ribbon: 1½ in (39 mm) wide, 1½ yds (1.40 m)
- Bottle green velvet tubing: ¾ yd (70 cm)
- Antique white double satin ribbon: 1½ in (39 mm), 4½ yds (4.15 m)
- Scarlet organza sheer ribbon: 1½ in (39 mm) wide, 9 yds (8.25 m)
- 5 stub wires
- 4 green leaves
- Pine sprigs, fresh or artificial
- 4 spruce cones, sprayed gold
- 12 gold ivy leaves

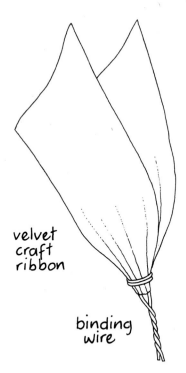

velvet craft ribbon

binding wire

1 Fold the wire-edged gold ribbon in half lengthwise and draw up the edging wires to shirr the ribbon.

2 Attach this ruched ribbon around the edge of the mat; stitching if it is straw or gluing if it is cork.

3 Fix the foam block to the centre of the mat with the plastic anchor and plasticine.

4 Tape the cocktail sticks to the candle, page 114, and place it centrally on the block.

5 Prepare and wire three double-looped cockades and two pairs of tails from the velvet craft ribbon, see diagram.

6 Prepare and wire four single bows from the green wire-edged ribbon, page 114.

7 Prepare and wire two double-looped bows from the velvet tubing.

8 Using the scarlet sheer ribbon on both sides of the white double satin ribbon, make up three ribbon roses and two buds on the stub wires, pages 115 and 116.

9 Arrange the green leaves and velvet tails around the base of the mat, firmly spiking the wires into the sides of the foam block, interspersing them with some of the pine sprigs.

10 Place one pine sprig centrally alongside the candle to mark the high-

point of the arrangement
and distribute the remaining
sprigs in the foam,
inserting them in outward-
pointing positions.

11 Wire the spruce cones,
page 115, and insert them
with the remaining
ribbon.

12 Position the roses and
buds, and arrange the gold
ivy leaves among the ribbons
to highlight the greenery.

13 Complete the arrangement by placing one of the
velvet loops centrally near
the candle and the second
towards the base.

GARLAND HITCHES

A trio of small cushions of Christmas colour that can form part of a corded garland, or be used individually to brighten a staircase or dark corner.

MATERIALS

- 2 dry florist's foam balls (1 ball makes two hitches): 3 in (7.5 cm) diameter
- 4 florist's plastic anchors
- Dressmaker's pins
- Gold holly and beech leaves
- Binding wire
- Green artificial holly sprigs
- Small pine sprigs with cones
- Scarlet single satin ribbon: ⅝ in (15 mm) wide, 3 yds (2.75 m)
- Gold ribbon: ⅝ in (15 mm) wide, 3 yds (2.75 m)
- Dark green double satin ribbon: ¼ in (6 mm) wide, 4 yds (3.70 m)
- Bleached achillea
- Small Christmas tree baubles
- Larch cones sprayed gold
- Scarlet silk cord: 3 yds (2.75 m)
- 5 brass rings: 1 in (25 mm) diameter
- Scarlet ribbon: ⅛ in (3 mm) wide, 12 in (30.5 cm)

1 Cut each foam ball in half.

2 Insert a florist's plastic anchor into the flat side of each half ball.

3 Pin individual gold leaves into the flat side around the outer edge, thus creating a circle of colour when the foam is placed on a flat surface.

4 Wire the holly and pine sprigs and insert them into the foam curve above the gold leaves.

3 Slip a ring on to the cord to point A, form a double loop with the end 30 in (76 cm) of the cord and stitch it to the ring.

4 Repeat this at the other end of the cord, at point C.

5 Using the narrow scarlet ribbon, or stitching if preferred, attach a second ring to each end ring.

6 Temporarily remove the florist's plastic anchor from the back of each hitch, slip a ring over one prong, and re-insert the anchor into the foam, so that one hitch is placed centrally and the other two hitches are placed over the cord loops.

To attach the hitches to a wall, beam or staircase, either singly or as a garland of three, use stick-on pads recommended for wall surfaces.

5 Using the scarlet ribbon, make 24 ribbon roses, page 115. Wire the gold and green ribbons into twelve double bows, page 114.

6 Continue inserting the remaining trimming in concentric rings, varying the colours and textures for greatest contrast.

7 Complete each cushion with a gold-sprayed larch cone placed centrally.

TO CONVERT THE HITCHES INTO A GARLAND

1 Mark the following measurements on the length of cord, see table below.

2 Sew a brass ring half-way along the cord length at point B.

----------------- A -------------	B -----------	C ----------------
30 in (76 cm) 24 in (61 cm)	24 in (61 cm)	30 in (76 cm)

· 2 ·
LIVING ROOM

Very often the living room
is the main focal point in
the home at Christmas
time. It is nearly always
where the tree is placed
and this can be trimmed in
many different ways –
maybe with lots of ribbon
bows and baubles in just
one or two colours, or with
a variety of decorations
collected over the years
which bring back memories
as they are unpacked each
Christmas.

·

There are several ideas in
this chapter for making
new trimmings for the tree.
There are also table and
hanging decorations,
a candy calendar and
stockings. The 'quick to
make' fabric table centre
gives a perfect background
setting for the special
candle table decoration.

᠅ CANDY CALENDAR ᠅

An unusual Advent calendar. Starting on December 1st, undo a ribbon bow, beginning at the bottom, and have a piece of candy every day until Christmas.

MATERIALS

- Scarlet double satin ribbon: 2¾ in (68 mm) wide, 2⅜ yds (2.20 m)
- Paper-backed adhesive: 2½ in (63 mm) wide, 41 in (104 cm)
- 1 cocktail stick
- Flat lace: ½ in (13 mm) wide, 2⅜ yds (2.20 m)
- Forest green double satin ribbon: ⅛ in (3 mm) wide, 2¾ yds (2.50 m)
- Thread
- Tartan ribbon: ⅜ in (9 mm) wide, 10 yds (9.15 m)
- 1 gilt bell
- 24 pieces of wrapped candy or similar sweets
- 1 tartan ribbon bow
- 1 gold lamé ribbon bow

---

1 Mark the centre of the length of the widest ribbon with a tailor's chalk line across the width.

2 Press the paper-backed adhesive strip to the ribbon, placing it up to the marked line, following the manufacturer's instructions.

3 Fold the ribbon over at the centre, aligning the edges carefully, and bond the two layers together, following the manufacturer's instructions.

4 Thread the cocktail stick in at the fold of the ribbon at the top, ensuring that it is ¼ in (6 mm) smaller than the width of the ribbon.

5 Cut the bottom to shape as shown in the diagram.

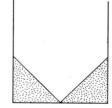

cut away shaded areas

6 Turn the raw edge of the lace under and place it over the edge of the ribbon.

Starting at the top and making a fold in the lace as the corners are reached, hold in position and machine with a zigzag stitch.

7 Overlay the edge of the lace with the ⅛ in (3 mm) ribbon and zigzag in place with a matching thread, making a fold at the corners as in Step 6.

8 Mark the spacing for the candy ties, starting 3 in (7.5 cm) from the top and then at 1½ in (3.8 cm) intervals. The last one should be about 3 in (7.5 cm) from the point at the bottom.

9 Divide the tartan ribbon into 24 pieces. Machine the ties in place with a small, close zigzag stitch.

10 Thread a 3 in (7.5 cm) length of the ⅛ in (3 mm) width ribbon through the ring of the bell, and stitch to the back at the point.

11 Stitch a 9 in (23 cm) length of the ⅛ in (3 mm) ribbon to the top.

12 Tie the pieces of candy or similar sweets in place and stitch the bows in position at the top.

✄ FABRIC TABLE CENTRE ❧

A very quickly made fabric mat for the centre
of a table, which makes an ideal setting for a bowl
of fruit or an arrangement of greenery
around a candle.

MATERIALS

- ↗ One printed cotton fabric panel designed to make a wreath
- ↗ Charcoal, light iron-on interfacing
- ↗ Thread

---

1 Cut out the two pieces on the printed outer line. Do not cut out the centre as for the wreath. Cut out two pieces of interfacing.

2 Press the interfacing to the wrong side of each piece with a damp piece of muslin and a medium-hot iron.

3 With the right sides facing, pin and tack the two pieces together,

matching the design on the edge carefully.

4 Machine stitch following the edge of the printed design, leaving an opening of 8 in (20 cm) for turning through.

5 Take out the tacking, trim the seam and snip towards the stitching on the curves and any dips if the panel has scalloped edges.

6 Turn right sides out and slip-stitch the opening to close. Roll the edges of the seam between the fingers and thumbs, tacking as you proceed. Press with a damp piece of muslin and a medium-hot iron. Remove the tacking.

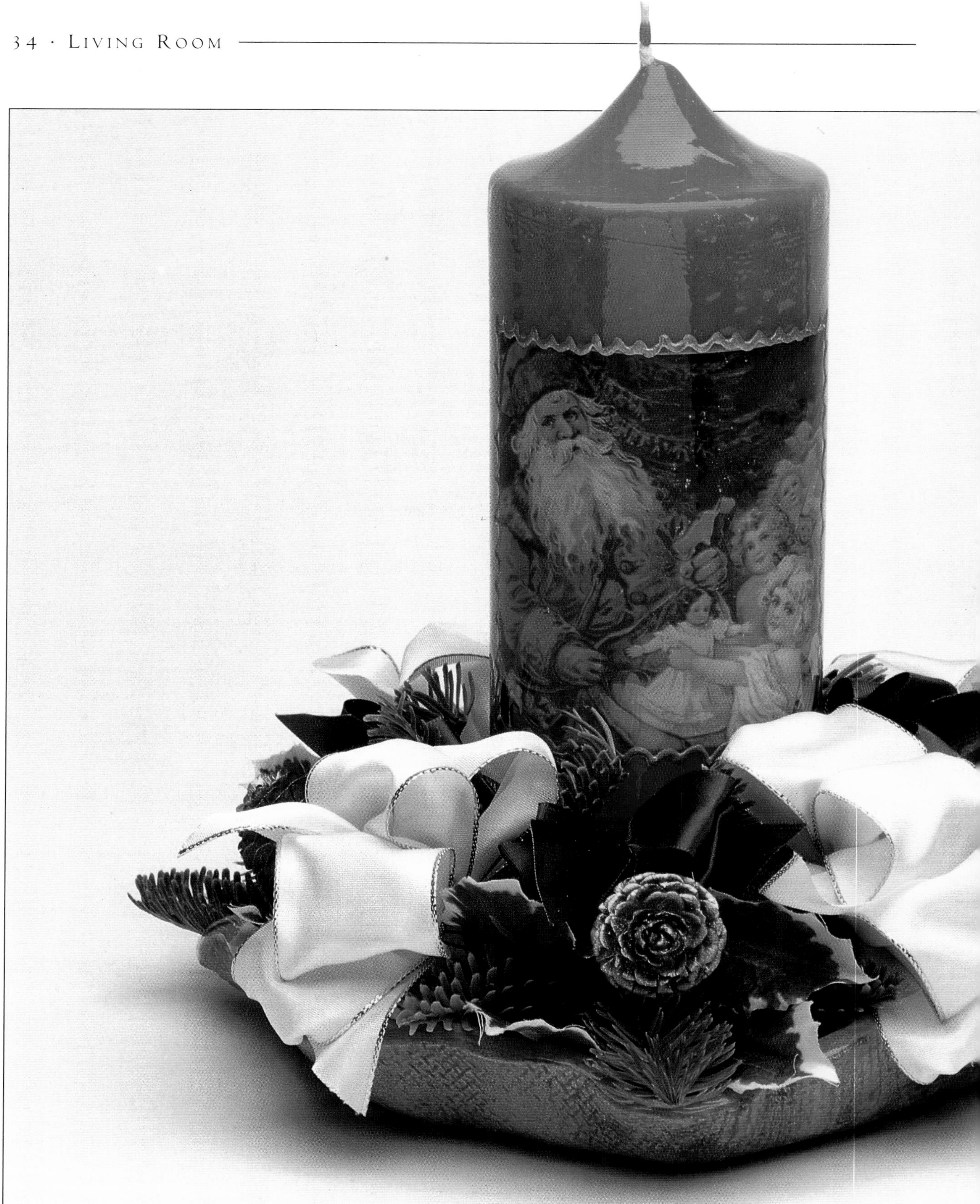

❧ CHRISTMAS CANDLE ❧

An ornamental candle to light you through the twelve days of Christmas.

MATERIALS

- Florist's plasticine fix
- Florist's plastic anchor
- Square block of dry florist's foam
- Ceramic or brass plate: about 7 in (18 cm) diameter
- Gold-edged cream wire-edged taffeta ribbon: 1½ in (39 mm) wide, 3 yds (2.75 m)
- Forest green single satin ribbon: 7⁄8 in (23 mm) wide, 2¼ yds (2.10 m)
- Binding wire
- 4 larch cones, sprayed gold
- 8 sprigs spruce or pine
- 8 sprigs variegated holly
- Christmas candle: 7 in (18 cm) high x 2½ in (6.3 cm) diameter
- Glue gun

---

1 Using the plasticine and plastic anchor, fix the dry foam block to the centre of the plate.

2 Divide the cream and green ribbons into four equal lengths and wire a double bow from each length, page 114.

3 Wire the cones and greenery, page 115.

4 Insert one cream bow in each quarter of the block, pressing the wire stem into the side and arranging the loops so that they conceal the foam.

5 Fill the spaces between the cream bows with the holly and spruce sprigs, adding a larch cone in each quarter.

6 Place the candle on the top of the foam, securing it in place with hot glue.

7 Insert the green double bows around the base of the candle, adding more spruce or pine if necessary.

❧ CHRISTMAS TREE DECORATIONS ❧

A selection of different ideas for making decorations to adorn the tree; some are very quick and easy to make, others take a little longer when some sewing is required.

❧ PRETTY BAUBLES ❧

MATERIALS

- Pins
- Ribbons: variety of short lengths
- Cotton spun balls (or similar)
- Beads and sequins

1 Pin the end of a piece of ribbon to the top of a ball, wrap it around, pinning at the bottom before returning and re-pinning at the top (Fig. A). Cut off the surplus. Repeat this process several times, with a variety of ribbons but using the same two pins.

2 Pin bows top and bottom, also a loop at the top for hanging (Fig. B). Beads and sequins can be threaded on to these pins before pushing them into the ribbon and balls.

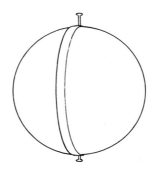

ribbon pinned to top

bottom pin

Fig. A

bows and hanging loop

bows

Fig. B

❧ HEART AND BELL ❧

MATERIALS

- Small pieces of fabric: 12 x 10 in (30.5 x 25.5 cm)
- Narrow ruffled lace: 1 yd (90 cm)
- Ribbon: ⅛ in (3 mm) wide, 1 yd (90 cm)
- Thread
- Polyester stuffing

1 Trace the templates, page 43, and cut out. For information on tracing templates see page 116.

2 Cut out two of each shape in fabric and apply lace to one piece of each, page 112.

3 Place a 6½ in (16.5 cm) length of ribbon for a hanging loop (Fig. A, page 38).

4 With right sides together, pin and tack the second piece of each to the appropriate shape.

Machine stitch with a ¼ in (6 mm) seam, leaving a 2 in (5 cm) opening for stuffing.

5 Snip the curved areas, and the dip at the centre top of the heart, taking care not to cut through the seam stitching (Fig. B). Turn right sides out.

6 Stuff both shapes to give a nice rounded appearance and slip-stitch the opening to close.

7 Trim both shapes with a bow on the front at the top.

Fig. A

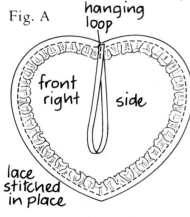

hanging loop

front right side

lace stitched in place

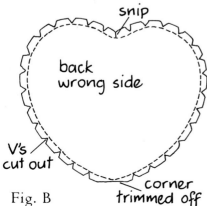

snip

back wrong side

V's cut out

corner trimmed off

Fig. B

❦ HANGING DIAMOND ❧

MATERIALS

- Thin card
- Small pieces of Christmas fabric
- Clear fabric glue
- Thread to match fabric
- Double satin ribbon: ⅛ in (3 mm) wide, 19 in (48.5 cm)
- 4 pearl-headed pins (optional)

---

1 Trace the template, page 43, and cut out in card. Additional information on tracing templates is given on page 116.

2 Cut out eight triangles in thin card. Place the template on the wrong side of the fabric, draw round, adding ½ in (1.3 cm) on all edges, and cut out eight triangles.

3 Place each thin card triangle centrally on the wrong side of the fabric triangles. Turn and glue the allowance down to the card.

4 Stitch four triangles together with a small oversew stitch, see diagram (right).

5 Cut a 10 in (25.5 cm) length of ribbon, fold and thread it through the point for a hanging loop.

Glue it on the inside to secure.

6 Stitch the remaining four triangles together in the same way. Thread short lengths of ribbon through the point to make a tail. Glue these on the inside.

7 Join the two pyramid shapes together by stitching the straight edge of a triangle from the top section to one on the bottom.

8 If liked, add pearl-headed pins around the centre where the points join.

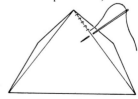

stitch four triangles together

For safety reasons make sure the decoration is out of reach of young children.

⋲ POT-POURRI PARASOL ⋩

1 Trace the template, page 43, and cut out. Additional information on tracing templates is given on page 116.

2 Cut out the shape in fabric. Turn under a 1/4 in (6 mm) hem on the curved edge, tack and press. Stitch lace to the hem on the wrong side.

3 Work a row of running stitches just below the lace. Do not fasten the thread off but leave a short length loose.

4 Fold the semi-circle in half, right sides together, stitch a 1/4 in (6 mm) seam, leaving a small opening near the fold (Fig. A). Press the seam open and turn right side out.

5 Push the pipe cleaner through the opening to protrude 3/8 in (1 cm) and slip-stitch the opening closed (Fig. B).

6 Fill the cone shape with pot-pourri up to the line of running stitches.

7 Pull up the gathering thread to close the cone shape and fasten off securely. Cover the gathering with ribbon, tying it in a bow.

8 Bend the top of the pipe cleaner over to form a handle.

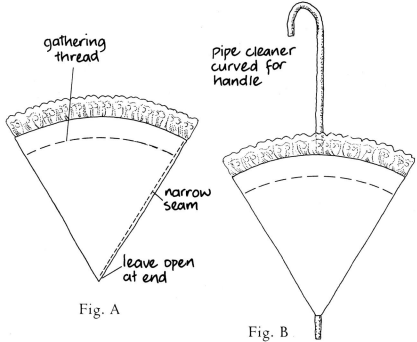

gathering thread

narrow seam

leave open at end

Fig. A

pipe cleaner curved for handle

Fig. B

LOLLIPOP
·: TIES :~

MATERIALS

- 2 lollipops
- Clear adhesive tape
- Tartan ribbon
- Narrow gold cord

1 Cross the lollipop stems and secure with a small piece of tape.

2 Trim with a tartan bow and hang on a gold cord.

·: MINI STOCKING

MATERIALS

- Patterned fabric: 6 x 9 in (15 x 23 cm)
- Light iron-on interfacing: 6 x 9 in (15 x 23 cm)
- Plain fabric: 6 x 9 in (15 x 23 cm)
- Thread
- Ribbon for trim, bow and loop

1 Trace the templates, page 42, of the stocking and cuff and cut out. Additional information on tracing templates is given on page 116.

2 Cut out two shapes for the stocking in patterned fabric, reversing the pattern as shown in the diagram, and two in interfacing. Cut out two shapes of plain fabric for the cuff.

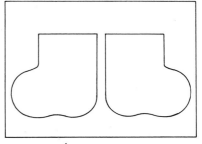

reversing the pattern

3 Press the interfacing to the stocking pieces, using a damp muslin and a medium-hot iron.

4 With right sides facing, pin, tack and machine the stocking with a $1/4$ in (6 mm) seam. Take out the tacking, trim the seam a little and cut V's round the outward curves.

5 Place the two pieces for the cuff right sides together and machine along the longest edge.

6 Turn to the right side and press. Zigzag stitch a ribbon trim along the edge. Stitch the cuff seam and press open.

7 Place the cuff over the stocking with the trimmed side to the wrong side of the stocking. Align the raw edges and stitch round.

8 Turn the stocking right side out and the cuff down.

9 Trim the back of the cuff with a bow and stitch a loop on for hanging.

❧ LITTLE ❧ BASKETS

Simple little willow baskets – so easily and quickly trimmed and filled with almost anything. The rims can be decorated with lace, ribbon woven around or through the sides, or small rosettes and ribbon bows tied or glued to the handle.

SUGGESTED MATERIALS FOR TRIMMINGS

❧ Lace and ribbon, gold cord

AND FILLINGS

❧ Small casuarina cones, sugared or almonds, sweets, nuts and raisins, small sprigs of dried flowers, immortelles, wild oats and sea lavender, pot-pourri and coloured berries.

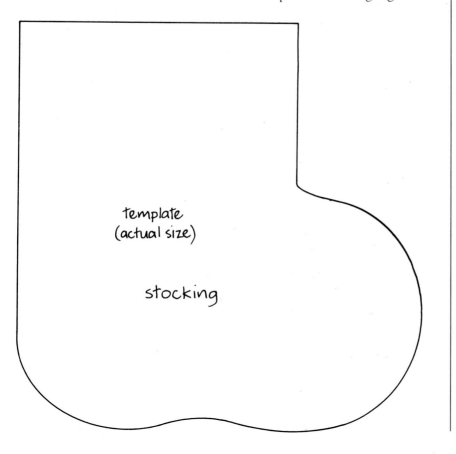

template
(actual size)

stocking

template
(actual size)

cuff

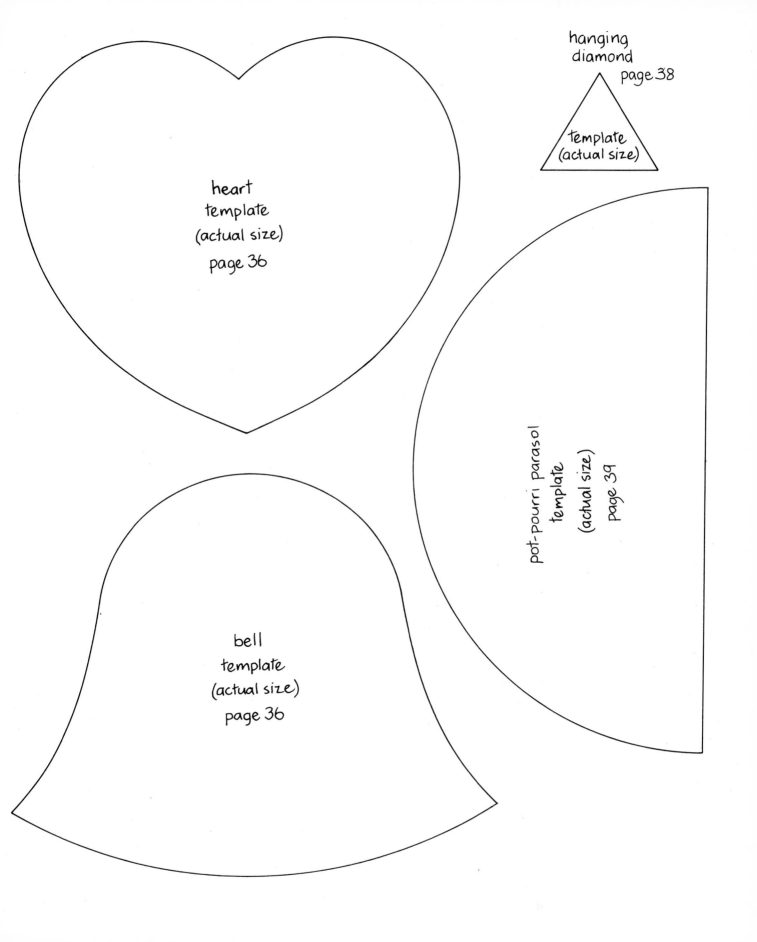

heart
template
(actual size)
page 36

hanging
diamond
page 38

template
(actual size)

pot-pourri parasol
template
(actual size)
page 39

bell
template
(actual size)
page 36

⤳ STOCKINGS ⤳

Christmas stockings can be made any size from mini to maxi, they can be made quickly and easily or be made in luxurious satin, quilted, beribboned and lined. There are also printed panels, that are available from craft fabric shops, with a variety of sizes from which to choose.

⤳ BASIC STOCKING ⤳
(MEDIUM-SIZE)

> ### MATERIALS
> ⤳ Fabric: 24 x 23 in (61 x 58.5 cm)
> ⤳ Ribbon: 5/8 in (15 mm) wide, 1½ yds (1.40 m)
> ⤳ Fusible web
> ⤳ Thread

1 Make the pattern for the stocking from the grid diagram, page 48. Additional information on using grid diagrams is given on page 117.

2 Cut out two shapes of fabric for the stocking and one for the cuff, placing this to a fold.

3 Place a ribbon trim on the toecap line of both stocking pieces, with fusible web underneath. Press in position with a medium-hot iron, laying a damp piece of muslin over the ribbon. With right sides together, pin and machine stitch ½ in (1.3 cm) from the edges, leaving the top open.

4 Trim the seam and snip inward curves, and cut V's out of the outward curves of the toe and heel. Do not turn right sides out at this stage.

5 Turn ½ in (1.3 cm) to the right side on the longest edge of the cuff to form a hem and press. Place fusible web inside, making sure it is completely covered, and press firmly using a damp piece of muslin and a medium-hot iron.

6 Press the ribbon trim along the hem of the cuff, and ¾ in (2 cm) from the raw edge as for the toecap (see Step 3).

7 With right sides together, stitch the back seam of the cuff and press open. Place the right side of the cuff to the wrong side of the stocking, aligning the back seam and raw edges. Stitch round ½ in (1.3 cm) from the edge.

8 Turn the stocking right sides out, and turn the cuff down on the edge of the ribbon trim. Sew an 8 in (20 cm) length of ribbon, folding it in half and turning the ends under to neaten for a hanging loop, to the inside on the back seam.

VARIATIONS
⤳ FUR CUFF ⤳

> ### MATERIALS
> ⤳ Fur fabric: 17 x 4 in (43 x 10 cm)

Make the stocking without the ribbon trim on the toecap line, following the basic instructions. Cut out the cuff without the bottom hem allowance, in fur fabric, making sure the pile will stroke downwards when in position. Attach the cuff and complete as before.

❧ QUILTED ☙ SATIN CUFF

As this cuff is fairly substantial, it is advisable to press a light iron-on interfacing to the stocking pieces before machining them together.

MATERIALS

- ↜ Satin fabric: 17 x 5 in (43 x 12.5 cm)
- ↜ Quilting backing: 17 x 5 in (43 x 12.5 cm)
- ↜ Thread, to match fabric and ribbon
- ↜ Double satin ribbon: $\frac{1}{8}$ in (3 mm) wide, 4 yds (3.70 m)

1 To make the cuff, cut out a piece of satin $17\frac{1}{2}$ x $5\frac{1}{2}$ in (44.5 x 14 cm). Press a quilting backing to the wrong side, according to the manufacturer's instructions. This backing has fusible trellis lines that can be followed for stitching on the $\frac{1}{8}$ in

(3 mm) ribbon. If it is not available, use a very thin wadding and cover with muslin on the back, tacking it in position; then draw the trellis lines on the bias of the fabric, $1\frac{1}{4}$ in (3.2 cm) apart.

2 Stitch the ribbon along the lines with a zigzag stitch, working in one direction first, and then crossing in the other. The best results are achieved by holding the ribbon along the lines whilst machining.

3 When all the ribbon is in position, turn under $\frac{1}{2}$ in (1.3 cm) along one long edge and sew the single turn hem down with herringbone stitch (page 111).

4 Fold the cuff in half widthways, place the pattern to the fold and cut the back seam to shape.

5 With right sides together, stitch the back seam $\frac{1}{2}$ in (1.3 cm) from the raw edges. Finger-press to prevent flattening the quilting. Apply the cuff and complete as before.

❧ BASIC ☙ SMALL STOCKING
(LINED)

MATERIALS

- ↜ Patterned fabric: 16 x 12 in (40.5 x 30.5 cm)
- ↜ Lining fabric: 16 x 12 in (40.5 x 30.5 cm)
- ↜ Light iron-on interfacing: 16 x 12 in (40.5 x 30.5 cm)
- ↜ Thread, to match fabric and ribbon
- ↜ Double satin ribbon: $\frac{1}{4}$ in (6 mm) wide, 5 in (12.5 cm)

1 Make the pattern from the grid diagram (page 48). Additional information on using grid diagrams is given on page 117.

2 Cut out two shapes in each of the following: patterned fabric, lining and interfacing, remembering to reverse the pattern if cutting from single fabric.

3 Press interfacing to the wrong side of each patterned fabric piece.

4 With right sides together, machine stitch each patterned piece to a lining piece along the top of the stocking, with ¼ in (6 mm) seam, and press open, see diagram.

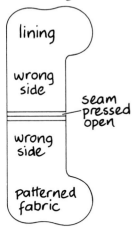

lining

wrong side

seam pressed open

wrong side

patterned fabric

5 Place the two halves right sides together, aligning the seams and raw edges, and machine round with ¼ in (6 mm) seam, leaving an opening of 3 in (7.5 cm) on the back of the lining. Snip inward curves and cut V's out round the toe and heel.

6 Turn right sides out and slip-stitch the opening to close.

7 Roll the seam of the stocking between fingers and thumbs, tacking as you proceed. Press with a damp piece of muslin and a medium-hot iron. Push the lining inside.

8 Fold a 5 in (12.5 cm) length of ribbon in half, and sew to the back seam.

VARIATIONS
GIFT CARD
❧ POCKET ❧

Follow the basic instructions Steps 1–3, then make the pocket as follows:

1 Cut the fabric in half, making two pieces 3½ x 2¾ in (9 x 7 cm). Press paper-backed adhesive to the wrong side of one piece with a dry iron. Allow to cool and peel off the backing.

2 Place the adhesive-side down over the second piece of fabric and bond the two layers together, using a damp piece of muslin under a medium-hot iron.

3 Cut the bottom of the pocket to a point, see diagram. Trim the top, sides and bottom of the pocket with ribbons, and gold cord. Zigzag stitch in place.

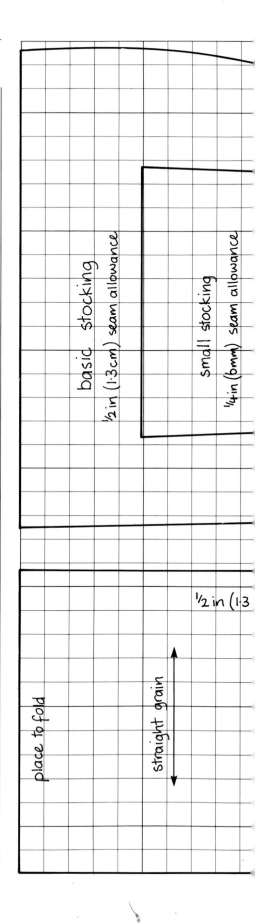

cut off the shaded areas

4 Position the pocket to one interfaced piece of stocking, 1¼ in (3.2 cm) from the raw edge at the top and ⅜ in (1 cm) from the edges.

Continue following the basic instructions Steps 4–8.

❧ QUILTED ❧
SATIN
STOCKING

Quilt the piece of fabric, page 46. Then follow the instructions for the basic small lined stocking.

basic stocking

½ in (1·3cm) seam allowance

small stocking

¼ in (6mm) seam allowance

½ in (1·3

place to fold

straight grain

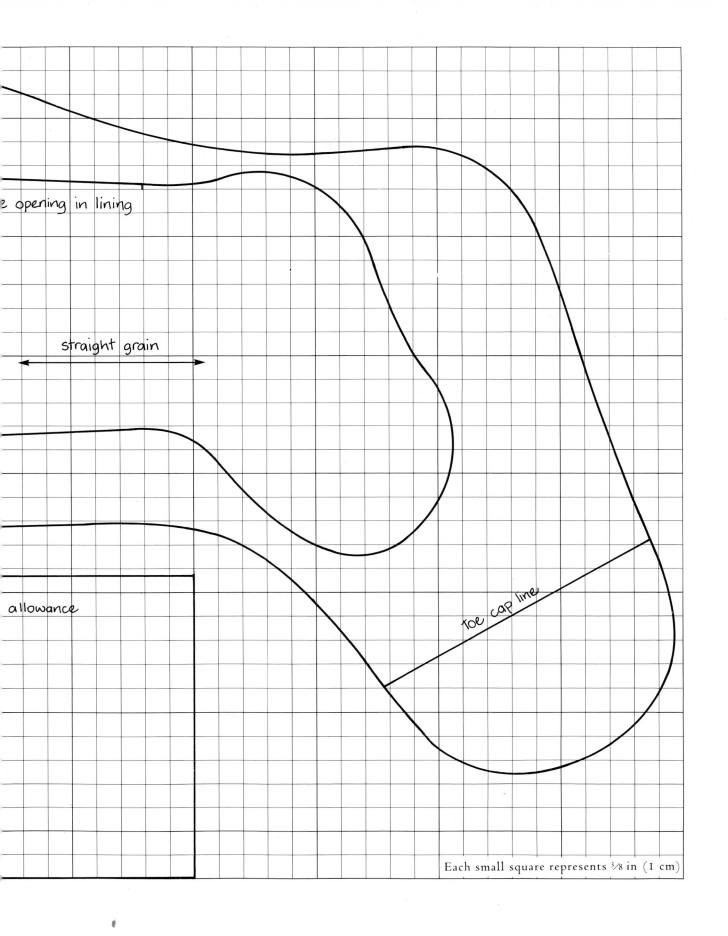

opening in lining

straight grain

allowance

toe cap line

Each small square represents ³⁄₈ in (1 cm)

· 3 ·
DINING ROOM

❧

Making table linen for Christmas, especially with the range of beautiful fabrics now available, will give pleasure from the moment the material is purchased to laying the table on the 'Day' and then waiting for your guests to sit down and admire the setting, with all the different extras that have been lovingly hand-made. The table setting has an underlay cloth for a rectangular table, place-mats, a present holder for the centre-piece, napkins with rings that match the candle holders, wine rings, bottle mats and wine glass coasters. A log cabin patchwork cloth is suggested for a square side table, and a special children's table setting uses a print fabric for the cloth which echoes the design on the ribbon-trimmed centre of sweets.

❧

❖ TABLE SETTING ❖

Making items for a full table setting requires forethought and planning. To 'bundle' the sewing processes of the place-mats, coasters and so on speeds up completion. The materials listed are for a six-place setting on a rectangular table measuring 60 x 36 in (152 x 91 cm).

MATERIALS

- Plain fabric: 45 in (114 cm) wide, 5 yds (4.60 m)
- Patterned fabric: 45 in (114 cm), 1¾ yds (1.60 m)
- Light iron-on white interfacing: 36 in (91 cm) wide, 2½ yds (2.30 m)
- Thread, to match colours used
- Crochet or embroidery cotton: about 10 yds (9.15 m)
- Ricrac trimming braid: 16 yds (15 m)
- Ribbon: ⅛ in (3 mm) wide, 2½ yds (2.30 m); contrasting colour 1⅜ yds (1.30 m)

MAKING PATTERNS

1 For the oval place-mats, fold a rectangular piece of paper, measuring 18 x 12 in (46 x 30.5 cm) into four. Pencil a mark 6 in (15 cm) from the corner of the longer side and, using the pencil and string method, page 117, draw an arc as shown (Fig. A) and cut out.

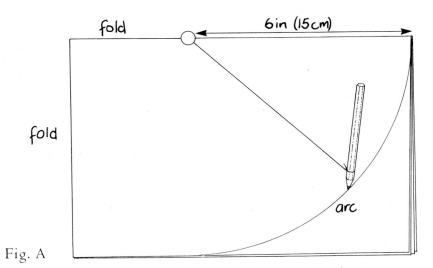

Fig. A

2 For the present holder, fold a 14 in (35.5 cm) square of paper into four, draw an arc as shown (Fig. B) and cut out. Using a pencil and ruler, divide the circular pattern into 12 equal segments (Fig. C).

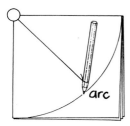

Fig. B

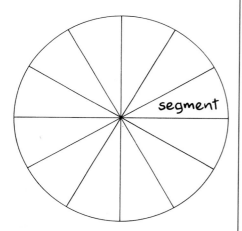

segment

Fig. C

3 For the wine mats and coasters, draw round a saucer or other suitable object of the required size: about 6 in (15 cm) circumference for the wine mats and 3¾ in (9.5 cm) circumference for the coasters. Cut out the patterns.

CUTTING OUT

1 From the plain fabric cut a 69 in (175 cm) length for the underlay (this will give a small overhang on all sides after hemming) and six napkins 18 in (46 cm) square.

2 Using the patterns, cut out the following from the plain and patterned fabrics and interfacing:
Oval Place-mats six plain, six patterned, six white interfacing
Present Holder three plain, three patterned, three white interfacing
Bottle Mats two plain, two patterned, two white interfacing
Coasters six plain, six patterned, six white interfacing

UNDERLAY CLOTH

1 Trim off the selvedges.

2 Make a narrow hem, turning ¼ in (6 mm) twice. Tack and press the hem both before and after machining.

NAPKINS

1 Turn ¾ in (2 cm) to the wrong side on the edges, pin and press the

fold. Turn ¾ in (2 cm) again and press. Form mitred corners, page 111.

2 Machine stitch the hems. Press.

3 To give a decorative finish to the hem on the right side, zigzag over a crochet cotton, or similar, with a matching thread. Use the stitching of the hem as a guide for the placement of the trim, and butt the edges of the crochet cotton as they meet.

PLACE-MATS, PRESENT HOLDER, WINE MATS AND COASTERS

1 Press white interfacing in position using a damp piece of muslin and a medium-hot iron to the wrong side of all the patterned fabric pieces.

2 Machine stitch the ricrac ¼ in (6 mm) from the edge of the right side of all the interfaced patterned fabric pieces. It is easier to get the placement correct by holding the ricrac in position while machining down the centre.

3 With right sides together, pin the plain fabric pieces to the trimmed patterned ones, placing pins as shown, see diagram.

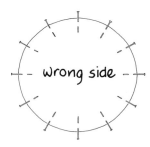

4 Tack round each item, removing the pins as you work. Machine stitch leaving a gap of 5 in (12.5 cm) for turning through the place-mat ovals and present holder circles, 4 in (10 cm) for the wine mats and 3 in (7.5 cm) for the coasters. Turning the work over before machining the pieces together will allow the stitching, from applying the ricrac, to be followed.

5 Remove the tacking, snip V's out of the larger items and trim the smaller ones close to the stitching. Turn right sides out, slip-stitch to close the gaps. Roll the seam to the edge between fingers and thumbs, tack as you proceed and press well with a damp

piece of muslin and a medium-hot iron.

To make up the Present Holder

1 Place the pattern on the plain fabric side of one of the circles and mark on every other line with tailor's chalk.

2 Stitch a 30 in (76 m) length of ribbon in place following the chalk lines, with a zigzag machine stitch, having an equal length protruding over the edges and placing an 8 in (20 cm) piece of contrasting coloured ribbon underneath each one near the edges, see diagram.

3 Replace the pattern on the same circle and mark on the lines that fall between each ribbon with tailor's chalk.

4 Place a second circle underneath so that the patterned sides will be together. Working from

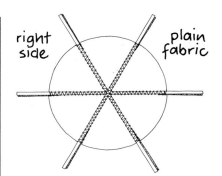

contrasting coloured ribbon placed underneath at the edges

the centre outwards, pin, then tack along the chalk lines, before machining with a zigzag stitch. Fasten the centre threads by pulling them through to the underside to knot together. The outer threads require threading in between the layers of fabric.

5 Turn the two joined circles over and place the third circle on top, plain fabric uppermost. Pin to prevent any movement and mark a 3 in (7.5 cm) line from the protruding ribbon lengths towards the centre. Tack along this line through the second and third circles only.

6 With the first ribbon-trimmed circle uppermost, machine along the tacked lines, starting from the outside and pulling back the first circle as you proceed to stitch the second and third together. Reverse stitch to secure at the beginning and end of each line.

7 Give a final press. Pull the ribbon ties to the centre to meet the opposite ones and tie together, ready to be filled with presents. Leave an extra length of ribbon on each present to attach a name tag which can be placed near each place-mat.

⌁TWO CANDLE HOLDERS⌁

Candles give the ultimate finishing touch to the festive table.

MATERIALS

- 2 cardboard rings: 2 in (5 cm) deep, 3 in (7.5 cm) diameter
- Scarlet craft ribbon: 2 in (50 mm) wide, ½ yd (45 cm)
- Clear adhesive
- 2 wooden coasters: about 3½ in (9 cm) diameter
- Narrow gold cord: ½ yd (45 cm)
- Dry florist's foam block
- 2 candles: 8 in (20 cm) high
- 8 cocktail sticks
- Clear adhesive tape
- Binding wire
- 40 artificial holly leaves
- 12 scarlet artificial holly berries
- 4 small wired bunches of pearl stamens
- Ivory single satin ribbon: ⅝ in (15 mm) wide, 2½ yds (2.30 m)
- Metallic ribbon: ⅛ in (3 mm) wide, 1¼ yds (1.15 m)
- Sprigs of sea lavender

1 Cover the outside of the cardboard rings with the scarlet craft ribbon, neatly sealing the ends with clear adhesive.

2 Glue the covered rings to the coasters.

3 Lay the gold cord round the base of each ring on the coaster and secure with glue.

4 Cut a piece of dry florist's foam to fit each ring and wedge it in firmly, making sure that the top is level with the edge of the ring.

5 Prepare the candles with the cocktail sticks for insertion into the foam, page 114.

6 Wire the holly leaves, berries and stamens.

7 Make six ribbon roses and six rosebuds on wire stems from the ivory ribbon, pages 115, 116.

8 Wire two treble loops of the metallic ribbon.

9 Set the prepared candles centrally in the foam-filled rings.

10 Arrange the trimmings around the candles, pinning each firmly into the foam and making sure that some of the leaves and sea lavender hang over the ribbon-covered edge of each holder. Complete the arrangements by inserting the metallic ribbon loops in the most effective position.

NAPKIN RINGS

A set of six to complement your Christmas table, matching the candle holders.

MATERIALS

- 6 cardboard rings: 1¼ in (3.2 cm) wide, 1⅞ in (4.8 cm) diameter (the inner tube from a roll of toilet paper will usually make three)
- Scarlet craft ribbon: 1¼ in (32 mm) wide, 2 yds (1.85 m)
- Clear adhesive
- Narrow gold cord: 2 yds (1.8 m)
- Ivory single satin ribbon: ⅝ in (15 mm) wide, 1¼ yds (1.15 m)
- Fine florist's wire
- Gold metallic ribbon: ⅛ in (3 mm) wide, 1 yd (90 cm)
- 12 small artificial holly leaves
- 6 small sprigs sea lavender
- 6 artificial holly berries
- 24 pearl stamens
- Florist's binding tape

1 Cover and line the six cardboard rings with the craft ribbon, securing with clear adhesive.

2 Glue the gold cord round the edges of the rings to cover the cardboard completely (Fig. A).

3 Using ivory ribbon, wire and make up six ribbon roses and six rose-buds, pages 115 and 116.

4 Divide the metallic ribbon into six equal lengths and wire six treble bows, page 114.

5 Wire all the remaining trimmings (Fig. B).

6 Assemble six small sprays in the hand from these trimmings, using the wire stem of the rose in each, to hold the group together.

7 Cut the grouped stems to a length of about 1 in (2.5 cm) and bind with florist's tape.

8 Glue a spray neatly to the point where the craft ribbon overlaps on each covered ring.

TWO WINE RINGS

Trimmed rings to slip on to wine bottles, to prevent any drops spoiling the special table linen. To get the perspective right, these rings are best worked 'in situ' on a bottle.

MATERIALS

- Clear adhesive
- 2 small pieces of sponge cloth: ½ in (13 mm) x inner circumference of ring
- 2 willow rings: about 3 in (7.5 cm) diameter
- Thread or binding wire
- Short lengths of ribbon, lace and beading
- Small cones, bells, berries and silk leaves
- 2 ribbon roses

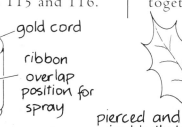

gold cord

ribbon overlap position for spray

gold cord

Fig. A

pierced and wired holly leaf

wired seed heads and holly berries

Fig. B

1 Glue the sponge cloth strips to the inner side of the rings, pressing firmly to the cane.

2 Stitch or wire the ribbon and lace into a double bow and cut the ends at a slant, page 114.

3 Place the bows on the upper side of the willow rings and glue in position.

4 Attach the beading towards the back of the ribbon bows so that the ends hang downward.

5 Add the remaining trimmings, inserting the leaves among the bow loops, placing any bells towards the front edge, berries towards the back and adding a ribbon rose, page 115, centrally to create a focal point on each ring.

⌒ LOG CABIN CLOTH ⌒

Traditionally log cabin blocks are visually divided diagonally by sewing strips of a light fabric to a central square on one side and of a dark fabric on the other. The log cabin patchwork pattern lends itself beautifully to the range of red and green Christmas fabrics that are readily available and by using several blocks, a cloth for a side table can easily be made. The instructions are for 16 blocks to be used to make a cloth measuring 41 in (104 cm) square.

MATERIALS

Use 45 in (114 cm) wide cotton fabric throughout and pre-wash and press before cutting out

- ⌐ Foundation fabric: 1¼ yds (1.15 m)
- ⌐ Plain red fabric for centre squares and backing: 1¼ yds (1.15 m)
- ⌐ 8 patterned Christmas fabrics (4 red and 4 green):
  Red:
  A and C: ¼ yd (25 cm)

E: ⅜ yd (35 cm)
G: ⅝ yd (60 cm)
Green:
B and D: ¼ yd (25 cm)
F and H: ⅜ yd (35 cm)

- ⌐ Dressmaker's pins
- ⌐ Thread to tone with fabric

CUTTING OUT

1 From the foundation fabric cut out 16 x 11 in (28 cm) squares.

2 From the plain red fabric cut out 16 x 2½ in (6.3 cm) squares.

3 From the red Christmas fabrics cut each length into 1½ in (3.8 cm) wide strips, label each design with the appropriate letter, A, C, E or G.

4 From the green Christmas fabrics cut each length into 1½ in (3.8 cm) wide strips, label each design with the appropriate letter, B, D, F or H.

TO MAKE ONE BLOCK

The stitching can be worked either by hand or machine and a ¼ in (6 mm) seam allowance is used throughout.

1 Using a pencil, mark the foundation square with the diagonal lines from corner to corner (Fig. A).

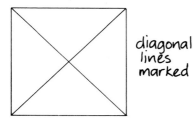

diagonal lines marked

Fig. A

2 Place a red square centrally on the foundation fabric and pin in place (Fig. B).

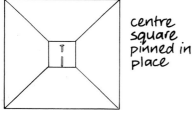

centre square pinned in place

Fig. B

3 Place a strip of fabric right side down over the centre square, ensuring the edges are even. Pin, trim to length and stitch in place. Remove the pin, fold the strip to the right side, finger press and pin again.

4 Working in a clockwise direction, lay another strip of fabric A over the centre square and the first strip, trim to the required length and stitch in place (Fig. C). Fold the strip to the right side, finger press and pin. Press with a warm iron, removing the pins as you proceed.

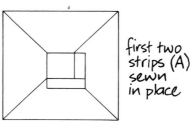

first two strips (A) sewn in place

Fig. C

5 Continue in a clockwise direction, place a strip of fabric B right side down over the centre square and the second strip. Stitch, fold and press as in Step 4. Place another strip of fabric B to enclose the central square, machine and press.

6 Using two strips of each fabric alphabetically and always working in a clockwise direction, add further strips as before, pressing after every two strips, until all the strips have been used ending with fabric H (Fig. D).

greens

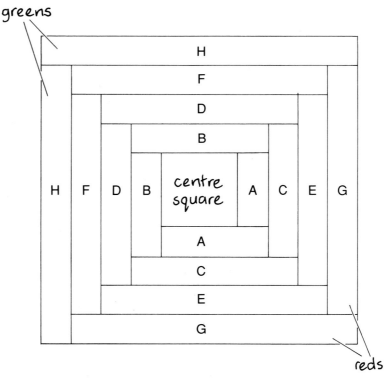

reds

Fig. D

7 Trim away any surplus foundation fabric. Make 15 more blocks in the same way.

Preparing and sewing several blocks at once saves time, especially where pressing is concerned.

To assemble the blocks

1 Arrange the blocks on a flat surface to achieve the desired effect, see diagram below.

2 Working in rows of together by stitching and pressing the seams open.

3 Join the four rows together, making sure all the seams are aligned. Press the seams open.

4 Cut a piece of backing fabric the size of the joined blocks. Place this right side down and lay the joined blocks over, right sides up. Pin in several places and tack the two layers together.

To bind the edges of the cloth

1 With right sides together, stitch a strip of fabric G to one side, trimming the ends off in line with the raw edges of the cloth. Press the binding and seam away from the cloth. Turn under the raw edge 1/4 in (6 mm), pin and slip-stitch to cover the stitching line.

2 Working in a clockwise direction as with the block, bind the remaining sides. The next two sides require a 1/2 in (1.3 cm) allowance at the beginning to neaten the previous corners; this allowance is turned in when the strip is slip-stitched down, see diagram below.

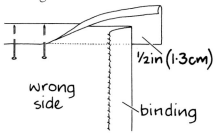

To bind the edges of the cloth

On the last side a 1/2 in (1.3 cm) allowance is required at both ends to neaten the corners. Give the cloth a final press.

To assemble the blocks

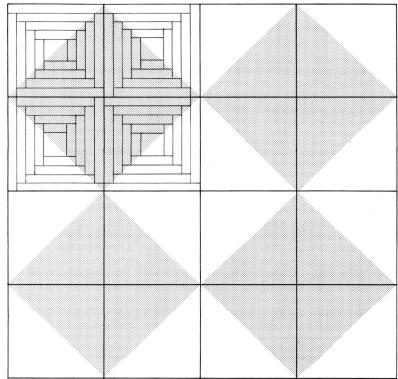

shaded areas denote the red strips

❧ CHILDREN'S TABLE SETTING ❧

Little ones love to have 'special things', so an easily made table-cloth, complete with a sweet centre, for their own table will surely please and bring instant smiles.

CHILDREN'S ❧ TABLE ❧ CLOTH

MATERIALS

❧ Fabric: calculate from table measurements

❧ Thread to tone with fabric

MEASURING

Measure the length and the width of the table, add 10 in (25.5 cm) to each measurement; this will give a small overhang of 4 in (10 cm) and allow for a double turn of ½ in (1.3 cm).

1 Form the hem as for the napkins, Steps I and 2, using the above hem allowance, page 54.

❧ CHILDREN'S ❧ SWEET RING

A teddy bear's 'picnic' of a table centre.

MATERIALS

❧ Cardboard tube: about 1½ in (3.8 cm) diameter, 6 in (15 cm)

❧ Scarlet craft ribbon: 1½ in (39 mm) wide, 5¾ yds (5.30 m)

❧ Clear adhesive

❧ Narrow gold cord: 1¼ yds (1.15 m)

❧ Dry florist's foam ring: 8 in (20 cm) diameter

❧ Double-sided adhesive tape

❧ White paper doyley

❧ Christmas print single satin ribbon: 1½ in (39 mm) wide, 3½ yds (3.20 m)

❧ Green double satin ribbon: ⅛ in (3 mm) wide, 24 in (61 cm)

❧ 8 sprigs of artificial holly

❧ 24 brightly coloured wrapped sweets

1 Cut the cardboard tube into four 1½ in (3.8 cm) lengths, page 115.

2 Line and cover each cardboard ring with scarlet craft ribbon, securing with glue.

3 Stick the gold cord carefully to the edges of the ribbon to cover any card that may be showing.

4 Cut four 9 in (23 cm) lengths of scarlet ribbon and place on one side.

5 Use the remaining ribbon to bind the dry florist's foam ring neatly, sealing the overlapped ends with double-sided adhesive tape. Place the ring on the doyley.

6 Cut the 1½ in (39 mm) Christmas print ribbon into four equal lengths. Fold each into a four-looped cockade, neatly stitching or tying at the base. Cut the ends at a slant.

7 Using double-sided adhesive tape, stick the four cockades in the four quarter positions on the ring, so that the crest of the first fold of each protrudes into the centre of the ring and the last fold sets at the outer base (Fig. A).

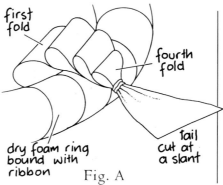

first fold

fourth fold

dry foam ring bound with ribbon

tail cut at a slant

Fig. A

8 Divide the green ribbon into four equal lengths and tie a bow round each cockade to cover the tie or stitching.

9 Tape or stick a covered tube to the top of the ring between each cockade.

10 Lay one of the four prepared lengths of scarlet ribbon over each tube so that the tail protrudes outwards on to the table (Fig. B) and secure to the tube with glue.

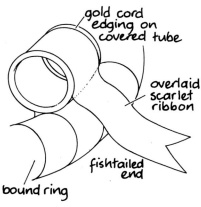

gold cord
edging on
covered tube

overlaid
scarlet
ribbon

fishtailed
end

bound ring

Fig. B

11 Cut the four ends of the scarlet ribbon into fishtails, page 115.

12 Pierce the ribbon covering either side of each cockade and insert a sprig of holly.

13 Using double-sided adhesive tape, attach an even number of sweets to each scarlet band.

Adhesive tape is used to attach the sweets to the ring for safety reasons.

∾ BABY'S BIB ∾

With the excitement of Christmas all around, a baby will know that everything is different, even the bib!

MATERIALS

- Fabric: 10 x 10 in (25.5 x 25.5 cm)
- Towelling: 10 x 10 in (25.5 x 25.5 cm)
- Thread to match the binding
- Bias binding (either purchased or made from fabric): 1 in (25 mm) wide, 1¾ yds (1.60 m)

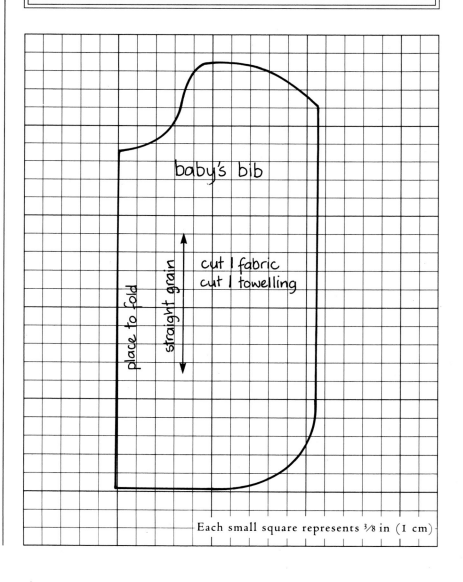

baby's bib

place to fold

straight grain

cut 1 fabric
cut 1 towelling

Each small square represents ⅜ in (1 cm)

CUTTING OUT

1 Make the pattern, following the grid diagram. Additional information on using grid diagrams is given on page 117.

2 Cut out one shape in fabric and one in towelling. Cut bias strips and prepare, page 112/114, if making the binding.

MAKING UP

1 With wrong sides together, tack the fabric and towelling pieces around the outer edges and neck.

2 Prepare the shape of the folded binding, by curving it to fit the outer edges. Curve the centre section of a 25 in (63.5 cm) length for the neck, leaving each end straight for the ties, page 114.

3 Bind the outer edges of the bib, slotting the raw edges into the fold of the binding, starting and finishing level with the neck edge. Machine with a zigzag stitch.

4 Mark the centre of the bib, and using the curved section on the prepared

length of binding, slot the raw edges of the neck into the fold of the binding. Tack into place, and along the folded edges to close the binding for the ties.

5 Machine the ties and around the neck with a zigzag stitch.

⌁ TODDLER'S TABARD ⌁

A tabard made in fabric that has an interesting Christmas design of toys and animals would be worn without protest!

CUTTING OUT

1 Make the pattern, following the grid diagram, page 70. Additional information on using grid diagrams is given on page 117.

2 Following the layout in the diagram, cut out the front, back and pocket. For the four ties, mark the dimensions on to the fabric, making each 8¾ in (22.5 cm) long by 1¾ in (4.5 cm) wide. Cut bias strips and prepare, page 112, if making the binding.

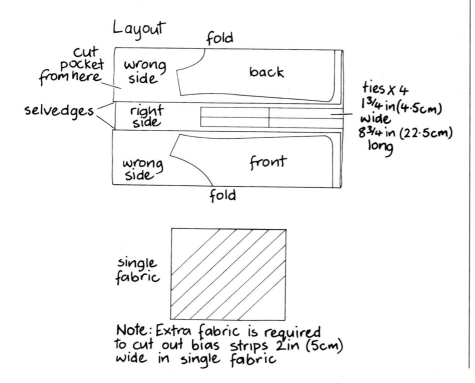

Layout

cut pocket from here

selvedges

fold

wrong side

right side

wrong side

back

front

fold

ties x 4
1¾ in (4.5cm) wide
8¾ in (22.5cm) long

single fabric

Note: Extra fabric is required to cut out bias strips 2in (5cm) wide in single fabric

MAKING UP

1 Mark the tie positions with tailor's tacks.

2 Join the shoulder seams with a run-and-fell seam, page 111.

3 Bind the top of the pocket, slotting the fabric into the binding, making sure the raw edge is to the fold. Machine with a zigzag stitch.

4 Position the pocket to the front of the tabard, aligning the raw edges at the sides and bottom. Pin and tack. Mark a line down the centre of the pocket, pin on both sides and, with a straight stitch, machine on the line, reverse stitching over the bias binding.

5 Make the ties; with right sides together, stitch across one end and along the length ¼ in (6 mm) from the raw edge. Turn right side out and press.

6 Prepare the shape of the folded binding by curving it to fit the neck and the edge around the tabard with a medium-hot iron, page 114.

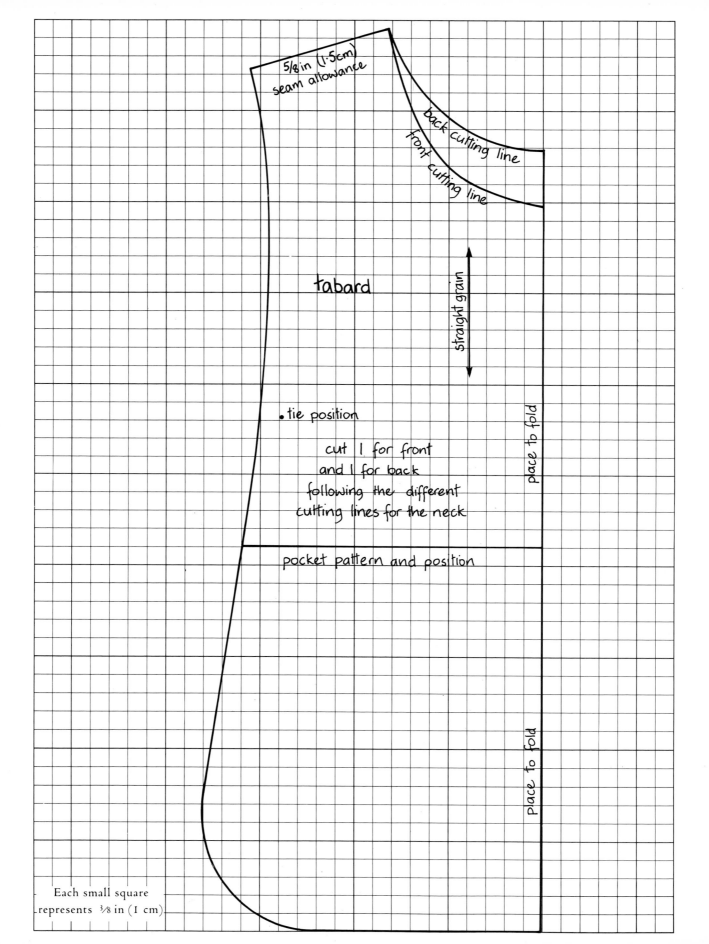

5/8 in (1·5 cm)
seam allowance

back cutting line
front cutting line

tabard

straight grain

• tie position

cut 1 for front
and 1 for back
following the different
cutting lines for the neck

place to fold

pocket pattern and position

place to fold

Each small square
represents ³⁄₈ in (1 cm)

7 Bind the neck, slotting the raw edge into the fold of the binding. Machine with a zigzag stitch, overlapping and turning in the raw edge to neaten the join.

8 Pin and tack the ties to the wrong side on the marked positions, having the fold edge upwards, see diagram.

ties tacked in position

back
wrong side

front
wrong side

neck binding machined
with zigzag stitch

9 Apply the binding, as in Step 7, to the outer edge.

10 Bring the ties over the binding and stitch with a zigzag stitch. Give a final press with a damp piece of muslin and a medium-hot iron.

⁓ TABLE-CLOTH ⁓

Use a very bright colourful fabric with a distinct pattern and then only the simplest construction is necessary to make this quick and easy table-cloth.

MATERIALS

↪ Fabric: calculate from table measurements

↪ Thread: to tone with fabric

MEASURING

Measure the length and width of the table and add 18 in (46 cm) to both measurements; this will give an average overhang of 8 in (20 cm) and allow for a double turn hem of $\frac{1}{2}$ in (1.3 cm) all round.

1 Form the hem as for the napkins, Steps 1 and 2, page 54, using the above hem allowance.

· 4 ·
KITCHEN

The kitchen at Christmas
time is always very busy
and full of activity preparing
and cooking the extra
goodies, as well as the
traditional dinner. It is,
however, often neglected as
far as decoration and items
for use at the festive time
are concerned.
The decorations, of course,
require to be in keeping,
and the spice ring and
bouquet garni plait do just
that, in an unusual way.

·

Using co-ordinating fabric
for 'HIS' and 'HERS'
aprons and oven mitts adds
that extra touch of
Christmas colour.

ꞈ SPICE RING ∾

This is a ring of friendship and the traditional gift of a country housewife, which evokes the warmth of the fireside and the scents of Christmas.

MATERIALS

- ꞈ Firm but lightweight card: 15 in (38 cm) square
- ꞈ Clear adhesive
- ꞈ Narrow gold cord: 5 in (12.5 cm)
- ꞈ Gold ricrac: 1⅛ yds (1.05 m)
- ꞈ Whole dried spices: allspice (pimento), bay-leaves, yellow split peas, cloves, star anise, stick cinnamon, mustard seed, white and green cardamom, black and green peppercorns.
- ꞈ Gold spray
- ꞈ Cinnamon single satin ribbon: ⅝ in (15 mm) wide, ½ yd (45 cm)
- ꞈ Light lacquer or hairspray

1 Cut out two 7 in (18 cm) diameter circles from the card. Cut out a 5 in (12.5 cm) diameter circle within each, thus leaving a 1 in (2.5 cm) wide ring.

2 Glue the two card rings together, enclosing the ends of the gold cord at the outer edge to create a hanging loop. Glue ricrac around the face of the ring, along the outer edge and around the back of the ring along the inner edge (Fig. A).

3 Spray some of the allspice (pimento) gold. Starting from the inside edge, glue a pattern of spices along the face of the ring, leaving spaces for small focal arrangements at the centre top and bottom. Alternate the spices to achieve the greatest colour and texture contrast. Add cardamom florets on each side of the ring, centering each flower with a clove, and a few small bay-leaves (Fig. B).

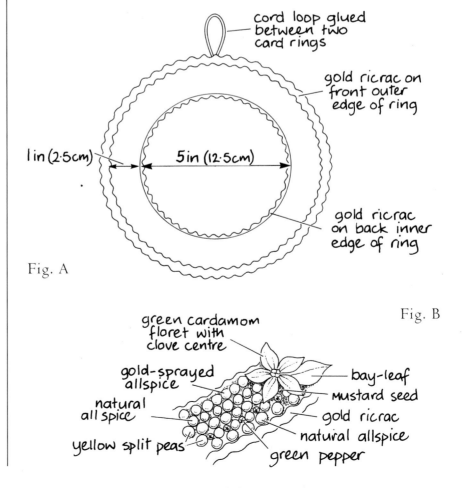

cord loop glued between two card rings

gold ricrac on front outer edge of ring

gold ricrac on back inner edge of ring

1 in (2.5 cm)   5 in (12.5 cm)

Fig. A

Fig. B

green cardamom floret with clove centre

gold-sprayed allspice

natural allspice

yellow split peas

bay-leaf

mustard seed

gold ricrac

natural allspice

green pepper

4 At the centre top and bottom of the ring, cover the card with mustard seed, then group the star anise and some of the cardamoms to simulate flowers and glue firmly in place.

5 Intersperse the florets with bay-leaves and small pieces of stick cinnamon. Centre each anise with a yellow split pea and each cardamom flower with a clove (Fig. C).

6 Make a double bow of ribbon and place this in the top focal group, adding more spices if necessary (Fig. D).

7 Spray with lacquer to set the spices and to add shine.

white cardamom floret with clove centre

green cardamom floret with clove centre

bay-leaf

star anise with split pea centre

Fig. C

cinnamon stick

hanging loop

double bow

white cardamom floret with clove centre

star anise with split pea centre

Fig. D

❧ BOUQUET GARNI PLAIT ❧

A plait of bouquet garni served with ginger, bay and nutmeg, with a tartan trim, colourful for the gourmet cook's kitchen.

MATERIALS

- Muslin: 6 x 36 in (15 x 91 cm)
- Scarlet double satin ribbon: ¼ in (6 mm) wide, ¾ yd (70 cm)
- Bouquet garni
- 12 white paper balls: ⅝ in (15 mm) diameter
- 12 cocktail sticks
- Clear adhesive or a little egg white
- Ground spices in four different colours, such as cinnamon, paprika, ginger and turmeric
- Bay-leaves, nutmegs, root ginger, cinnamon bark or sticks
- Straw plait: about 14 in (35.5 cm) long
- Tartan ribbon: 1½ in (39 mm) wide, 1⅝ yds (1.50 m)
- Forest green velvet craft ribbon: 1½ in (39 mm) wide, ⅝ yd (60 cm)

---

1 Cut the muslin into six 6 in (15 cm) squares. Cut the scarlet ribbon into one 3 in (7.5 cm) and six 4 in (10 cm) lengths.

2 Place a spoonful of bouquet garni in each muslin square and tie with a length of scarlet ribbon to make up six sachets.

3 Spike the paper balls on the cocktail sticks, cover with adhesive, and roll three in each colour of the ground spices. Allow to dry.

4 Lay six large bay-leaves down the right-hand side of the straw plait and secure with a dab of glue or egg white. Allow to dry.

5 Lay the six sachets, tails to the left, down the straw plait and secure each one firmly to the plait with two of the topped cocktail sticks.

6 Cut a 22 in (56 cm) length of the tartan ribbon, and with the green velvet craft ribbon superimposed, fold and stitch the two into a single bow, page 114.

7 Cut an 8 in (20 cm) length of tartan ribbon, fishtail the ends, page 115, and put it on one side.

8 Fold the remaining tartan ribbon into a double bow and arrange the two bows at the base of the plait, stitching them or securing them with a tie.

9 Insert bay-leaves and cinnamon bark or sticks among the bow loops.

10 Arrange the root ginger and nutmegs centrally and secure with glue.

11 Tie the 3 in (7.5 cm) length of scarlet ribbon tightly round the 8 in (20 cm) length of tartan ribbon. Fold this in half and insert it neatly beneath the lowest bay-leaf, tying it in at the base of the plait, so that the two ends hang downward.

The completed plait can be sprayed with lacquer for gloss and a firmer hold. In this case the spices and bay-leaves should not be used for cooking.

For arrangements in the kitchen, for safety reasons, do not to use wire or pins. Use stitching, a tie or glue; for small light additions a dab of egg white is an alternative.

❧'HIS' AND 'HERS' APRONS❧

Quickly and easily made from the same pattern, 'HIS' has square corners on the pocket and hemline, which is in keeping with the tartan fabric; 'HERS' are rounded. All raw edges are neatened with binding from the fabric used for their partner's apron.

MATERIALS

There will be sufficient spare fabric to make the oven mitts.

- ❧ Fabric: 45 in (114 cm) wide, 2¼ yds (2.10 m) each of two mix-and-match designs
- ❧ Thread to match

CUTTING OUT

1 Make the pattern following the grid diagram (page 80). Additional information on using grid diagrams is given on page 117.

2 Following the layout in the diagram, place and pin the main piece and pocket to a fold. If you are using tartan or checked fabric, make sure the straight lines on the pattern, are on a line in the design; match up the design for the pocket, if possible too. Cut out these pieces.

3 Mark the length and width required for the strips to make the ties on to the fabric with tailor's chalk.

4 From single fabric, mark and cut bias strips for binding (page 112).

MAKING UP

1 Make the bias strips into binding, page 114.

2 Bind the pocket in the following order: 'HIS': the bottom, the sides, the top; 'HERS': the sides and curved bottom and the top. Slot the raw edges into the binding and machine in place with a zigzag stitch. Curve the binding where necessary, page 114, and turn under the end raw edges of the binding when overlapping the previous piece.

3 Taking the position from the pattern, place the pocket on the apron piece. Pin and tack. Machine over the edge of the binding on the sides and bottom with zigzag. Remove the tacking.

4 Mark a centre line on the pocket with tailor's chalk, pin both sides to prevent any movement and machine with a straight stitch, reversing the stitching at the beginning and end.

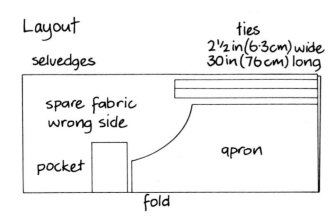

Layout

ties
2½ in (6·3cm) wide
30 in (76cm) long

selvedges

spare fabric
wrong side

pocket

apron

fold

Mark and cut bias strips
2in (5cm) wide from single fabric
using the spare fabric

5 Bind the outer edges in the following order: 'HIS': the bottom, the sides, the armhole edges and the top; 'HERS': the sides and curved bottom, the armhole edges and the top. Apply and curve the binding as for the pocket.

6 To make the ties, with right sides together, stitch across one end and along the length ¼ in (6 mm) from the raw edges. Turn right sides out and press.

7 Turn the raw edge under ⅜ in (1 cm) on each tie and position them as marked on the pattern. Adjust the length of the ties at this stage if necessary. Tack in place and machine stitch.

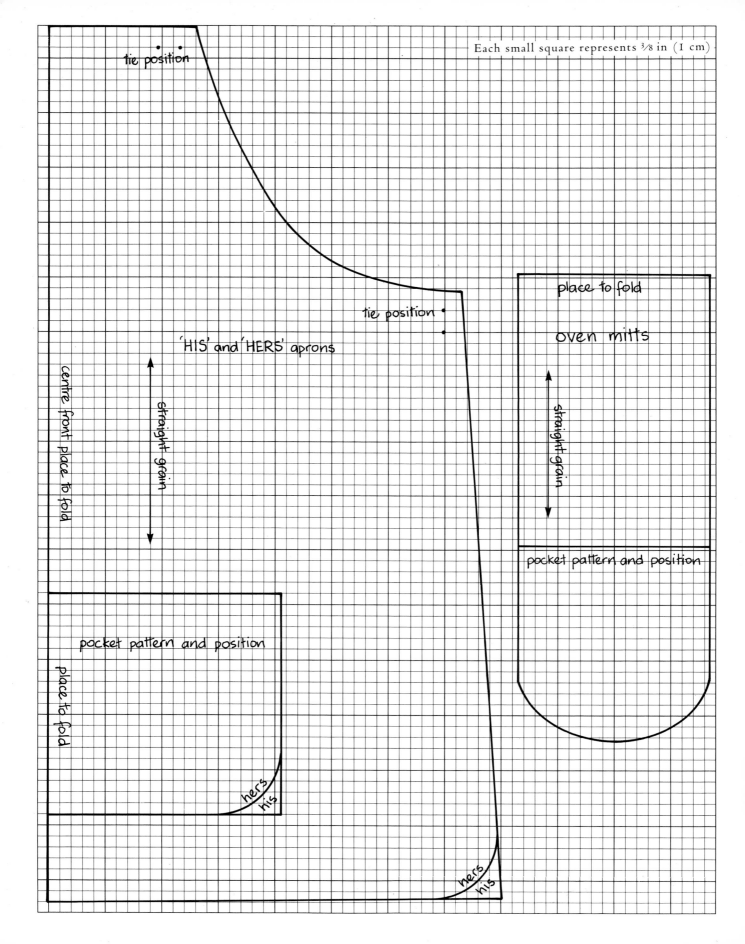

Each small square represents ⅜ in (1 cm)

tie position

tie position

'HIS' and 'HERS' aprons

oven mitts

place to fold

centre front place to fold

straight grain

straight grain

pocket pattern and position

place to fold

pocket pattern and position

hers
his

hers
his

❧ OVEN ❧ MITTS

Really essential and much safer than a cloth, made in a nice bright colour, they will be easily found when put down! Spare fabric from other projects could be used for this item.

MATERIALS

- ❧ Fabric (main colour): 1 piece 34 x 8 in (86.5 x 20 cm); 1 piece 20 x 15 in (51 x 38 cm)
- ❧ Fabric (co-ordinating colour): 1 piece 34 x 8 in (86.5 x 20 cm)
- ❧ Light iron-on charcoal interfacing
- ❧ Thick wadding (check that it is suitable for holding hot dishes)
- ❧ Bias binding (either purchased or made from fabric): 1 in (25 mm) wide, 2¾ yds (2.50 m)

CUTTING OUT

1 Make the pattern following the grid diagram, opposite. For information on using grid diagrams see page 117.

2 Cut out the main piece in each of the fabrics.

3 Cut four pockets, two on the bias and two on the straight grain for lining. Cut out two in interfacing.

4 Cut bias strips and prepare, page 112/114, if making the binding.

MAKING UP

1 Press interfacing to the bias pieces of the pockets with a damp piece of muslin and a medium-hot iron.

2 With wrong sides together, pin and tack the pocket linings to the interfaced pocket pieces.

3 Bind the top of the pockets, slotting the fabric into the binding, making sure the raw edge is towards the fold. Machine with a zigzag stitch.

4 Lay one main piece of fabric right side down, place the wadding on top and lay the second main piece over the wadding right side up.

5 Secure the layers together with a few pins.

Working from the centre outwards, tack as shown in the diagram. Do not pull the tacking thread tightly.

6 With a large machine stitch, work lines of stitching to quilt the prepared piece, using the design where possible. Alternatively, mark lines, using a ruler and tailor's chalk or fabric pen.

7 Tack around the outer edges ⅝ in (1.5 cm) and trim the wadding away a little from the raw edges. Machine stitch with a zigzag stitch over the raw edges.

8 Position the prepared pockets on the ends of the quilted piece, aligning the raw edges, pin and tack.

9 Prepare the shape of the binding by curving it to fit round the curves at each end, page 114.

10 Slot the raw edges into the fold of the binding and tack in place, overlapping and turning under the end raw edges to neaten the join. Machine with a zigzag stitch. Remove the tacking and press binding edges only.

· 5 ·
BATHROOM

A touch of Christmas in
the bathroom is a pleasant
surprise! Children especially
will like having their own
guest towel. The basket of
toiletries will not only help
to keep the bathroom tidy
at this busy time, but will
also give a choice of an
enticing selection of soaps
and bubble baths.
The toilet roll holder is
different – and it
complements the basket
lining. The unusual straw
circle to hold scented and
softening bath sachets,
with their trim of holly
and berries, will give a
touch of brightness to the
bathroom.

TRIMMED GUEST ❧ TOWELS ❧

Quickly and easily trimmed with festive ribbon, purchased to 'fit' the border which is found on most towels.

MATERIALS

- Light iron-on interfacing, sufficient to back the ribbon
- Ribbon: width and length of the border x 2 + 1 in (25 mm) for each towel
- Tack stick (a light glue which washes away)
- Thread to match the ribbon and towels

---

1 Press the interfacing to the wrong side of the ribbon, taking care that it is within its width.

2 Apply tack stick to the interfaced back and place the ribbon over the border of the towel, turning the ends under ½ in (1.3 cm) at each end.

3 Using a zigzag stitch, machine along both edges, working in the same

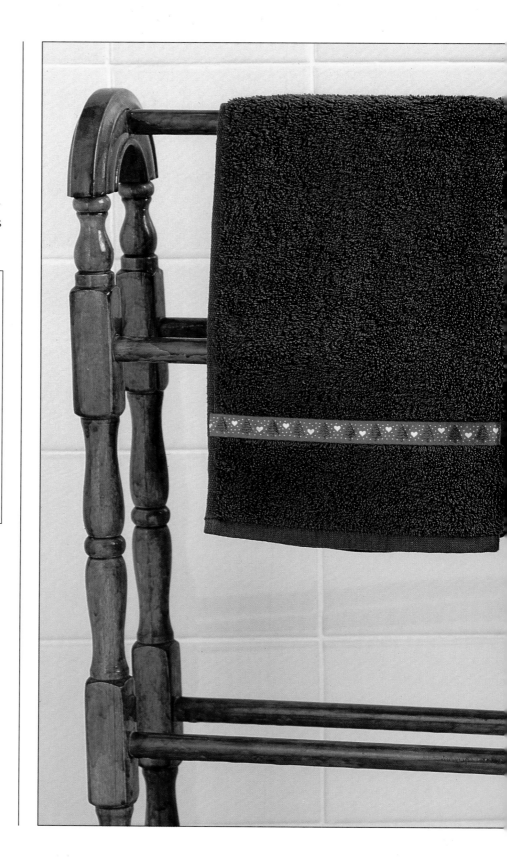

direction. Stitch the ends securely. If the towel is in a contrast shade to the ribbon trim, use the appropriate thread shade in the bobbin.

∴ LINED ∾ BASKET FOR TOILETRIES

Baskets can be purchased in many shapes and sizes and to calculate the fabric required, they have to be measured. Always note the figures down as you are measuring.

MATERIALS

- ↻ Basket
- ↻ Cardboard: medium thickness
- ↻ Paper-backed adhesive
- ↻ Craft interfacing
- ↻ Fabric: two contrasting shades
- ↻ Thread to match fabric
- ↻ Ribbon: perimeter measurement plus 1 yd (90 cm) in each shade

---

MEASURING

I Measure the side from the inside and add 1 1/2 in

(3.8 cm); this gives the depth cutting measurement and allows for a seam allowance of ¼ in (6 mm) at the top, ½ in (1.3 cm) at the bottom, and ¾ in (2 cm) above the drawstring casing to form a ruffle.

2 Measure the perimeter from the outside, at the top of the basket, and add half this measurement, plus 1½ in (3.8 cm). The total gives the measurement for the cutting length of the side.

MAKING UP

1 Stand the basket on a piece of paper to make a pattern for the base and draw around.

2 Cut out the pattern and try it for size; it needs to sit easily on the bottom of the basket. Trim it if necessary. Cut out the same shape in cardboard; this will be placed permanently in the bottom.

3 Draw around the cardboard shape on the paper-backed adhesive. Press this on to the craft interfacing, using a dry iron directly on to the paper (making sure that the interfacing is larger than the adhesive paper). Allow to cool and cut out the shape. Peel off the paper.

4 Place this shape, adhesive-side down, on to the wrong side of a larger piece of main colour fabric and press, following the manufacturer's instructions.

5 With tailor's chalk, mark on the fabric a ½ in (1.3 cm) seam allowance, and cut on the line.

6 Cut the side strips, one in the main and one in the contrast fabric. Cut both in half widthways.

7 Machine stitch the two seams in both the main and contrast fabrics with ⅜ in (1 cm) seams. Press open.

8 With right sides facing, join the strips together with a ¼ in (6 mm) seam, having aligned the seams of one strip with the other. Turn right sides out. Roll the seam between fingers and thumbs to bring it to the edge, tacking as you proceed. Press the edge using a damp piece of muslin under a medium-hot iron.

9 Tack the two layers together, aligning the seams and raw edges of the bottom of the strip.

10 Machine stitch to form the casing for the ribbon, ¾ in (2 cm) from the top edge and ⅜ in (1 cm) from the first line of stitching, using the appropriate thread top and bottom to match fabric.

11 Divide the length of the strip into four equal sections and mark with pins. With the main fabric side uppermost, and using a large machine stitch, work two rows of stitching for gathering, one ½ in (1.3 cm) from the raw edges and the other ⅛ in (3 mm) away from the first, having a break of threads at each pin. Pull all threads through to the contrast fabric side.

12 Divide the base into four equally and measure one section. Pull up the bobbin threads of both lines of stitching together, section by section, to correspond with the measurement of the base sections.

13 With right sides together, apply the gathered strip to the base. Place the pins across the gathers and use the ones that are marking the section divisions to wind the gathering threads round, figure-of-eight style; this will hold the threads taut enabling the gathers to be arranged evenly.

14 Probably the gathers will be very close, especially if the basket has sloping sides, so, to avoid having to take out the tacking after machining, tack using the machine sewing thread.

15 Machine stitch the side to the base, having the gathers uppermost, on the seam line and $1/8$ in (3 mm) away from the first; the gathering lines can be used as a guide. Trim very near to the second line of stitching.

16 Undo the seam between the casing lines on the contrast fabric side. Thread with ribbon, using shades to match the fabric, from seam to seam, allowing sufficient for tying to the handle or through the weave of the basket.

TOILET ROLL ∴ COVER ∾

A 'dolly' bag cover made to complement the style of the lined basket.

MATERIALS

↜ Fabric: two contrasting shades

↜ Light iron-on interfacing

↜ Ribbon for trim: $5/8$ in (15 mm) wide, length of calculated side x 2

↜ Ribbon for draw-strings: $1/8$ in (3 mm) wide, about $1^{3}/8$ yds (1.30 m) each of two contrasting shades

↜ Thread to match fabrics

MEASURING

1 Measure the height, diameter and circumference of a toilet roll and write them down.

2 Add the seam and ease allowance: for the base, 1 in (2.5 cm) to the diameter; for the length of the side cover, $2^{1}/2$ in (6.3 cm) to the circumference; and for the depth of the side calculate as follows: height + diameter.

CUTTING OUT

1 Make a pattern for the base using the calculated diameter measurement, page 117.

2 From the main fabric cut out the base using the pattern, and a strip for the side of the length and depth required.

3 From the contrasting fabric cut a strip 4 in (10 cm) wide by the length needed for the side.

4 Cut out interfacing for all pieces.

MAKING UP

1 Press interfacing to all pieces using a damp piece of muslin and a medium-hot iron.

2 Cut the main and contrasting fabric strips in half widthways.

3 With right sides together, machine the main fabric strips together with a $1/4$ in (6 mm) seam. Press open.

4 Apply the two ribbon trims, placing the first the width of the ribbon above the $1/4$ in (6 mm) seam allowance at the bottom of

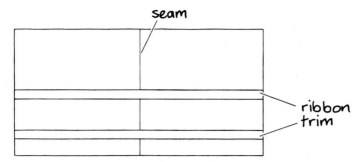

seam

ribbon trim

the side, and the second 1¾ in (4.5 cm) above. Press the ribbon in position using a fabric adhesive web underneath. Zigzag in place, see diagram.

5 Join the second seam to make the strip into a round, taking care to align the ribbon trims.

6 Stitch a line with a normal length machine stitch ¼ in (6 mm) from the raw edge at the bottom of the side. Snip at ½ in (1.3 cm) intervals towards the stitching.

7 With right sides together, stitch the side to the base along the seam line. Trim the seam a little and turn right sides out.

8 Stitch the seams of the contrast strip. Press open. Place this right sides together to the main fabric at the top of the sides, aligning the seams. Machine stitch ¼ in (6 mm) from the raw edges.

9 Turn the contrast to the inside, and roll the seam to the edge with fingers and thumbs, tacking as you proceed. Press the edge using a damp piece of muslin and a medium-hot iron.

10 Machine stitch the casing for the ribbon 1½ in (3.8 cm) from the top and ⅜ in (1 cm) from the first line of stitching.

11 Undo the machine stitch of the side seams between the casing lines. From one opening insert two contrasting lengths of ribbon completely around the top and knot to join; repeat with remaining two lengths from the other opening.

❧ SUN CIRCLE OF SACHETS ❧

A straw circle of muslin sachets filled with rosemary and oatmeal to scent and soften the bathwater.

MATERIALS

- ❧ Muslin: 12 x 30 in (30.5 x 6 cm)
- ❧ 10 tablespoons of mixed oatmeal and dried rosemary
- ❧ Strong white thread
- ❧ 10 small sprigs of artificial holly
- ❧ Scarlet double satin ribbon: ⅛ in (3 mm) wide, 2¾ yds (2.50 m)
- ❧ 1 wheat straw sun with ten broad rays: about 10 in (25.5 cm) diameter

---

1 Cut ten squares measuring 6 x 6 in (15 x 15 cm) from the muslin, and place a tablespoon of mixed oatmeal and rosemary in each, tying firmly with thread.

2 Insert a holly sprig into the centre of each.

3 Cut a 6 in (15 cm) length of scarlet ribbon and form a hanging loop on one point of the straw sun.

4 Divide the remaining ribbon into ten equal lengths. Loop each length through the centre of the sun and tie round a sachet, positioning one sachet between each straw ray.

· 6 ·
BEDROOMS

It gives pleasure and
enjoyment to prepare for a
guest at Christmas time,
whether it is a member of
the family or a friend.
Special pretties in fabric
with a design in festive
colours make a thoughtful
welcome on entering the
bedroom, especially if they
are items that will be used
throughout the visit.

·

For the bedside table,
a lace-trimmed tissue box
cover, covered hangers and
scented sachets for the
wardrobe, and, to serve
morning tea, a breakfast
set, consisting of a tray
cloth, napkin and tea cosy,
made in the same fabric.
A basket of ribbon roses
co-ordinates the items.

·

For the children's
bedroom, a wall hanging of
the Star of Bethlehem
patchwork design, and a
mobile made from fabric
tree decorations.

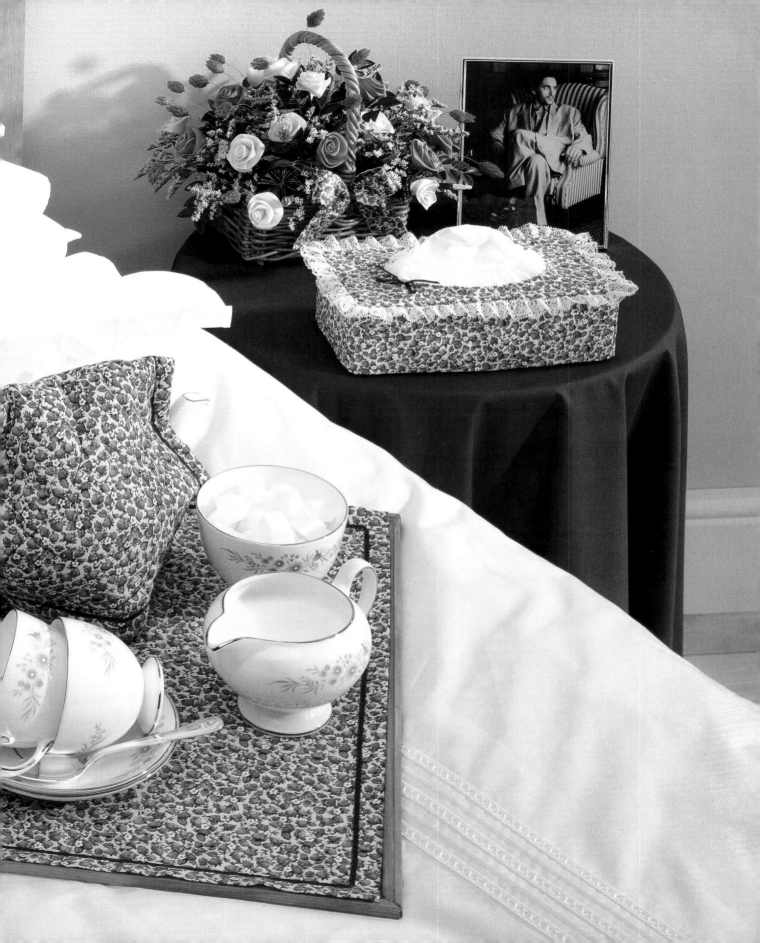

⌇ LACE-TRIMMED TISSUE BOX ⁓ & COVERED HANGERS WITH POT-POURRI SACHETS

It gives a little touch of luxury to have lace-trimmed items just waiting to be used.

MATERIALS

- Box of tissues: example used 9½ x 4¾ in (24 x 12 cm) x 2¾ in (7 cm) deep
- Two wooden hangers: 17 in (43 cm) long
- Fabric: 45 in (114 cm) wide, ½ yd (45 cm)
- Medium iron-on interfacing: two pieces, 10 x 5 in (25.5 x 12.5 cm) and 30 x 3 in (76 x 7.5 cm)
- Medium thickness wadding:

- 18 x 8 in (46 x 20 cm)
- Fabric pen
- Ruched lace: 1 in (25 mm) wide, 2 yds (1.85 m)
- Forest green double satin ribbon: ⅛ in (3 mm) wide, 1 yd (90 cm)
- 3 ribbon roses (purchased or hand-made), page 115
- Velvet tubing: 12 in (30.5 cm)
- Pot-pourri

Hangers
two fabric 6 in (15 cm) wide by required length, two wadding 4½ in (11.5 cm) wide by required length
Sachets
four fabric

TISSUE ⌇ BOX ⁓

1 Press the interfacing to one top and the side piece within the seam/hem allowance, using a damp piece of muslin and a medium-hot iron.

2 Place the two top pieces right sides together and pin.

3 Remove the perforated section from the top of the tissue box and place it centrally to the interfaced top piece. Draw around it with a fabric pen.

4 Tack a little way from the line, nearer to the outer edges.

5 Machine stitch on the

MEASURING

1 Measure the tissue box dimensions and write them down. Add the seam/hem allowance: for the top ¾ in (2 cm) to both the length and width; for the side length ¾ in (2 cm) to the perimeter, and to the side depth ⅞ in (2.3 cm).

2 Measure the length of the hanger, for the fabric cover add 6 in (15 cm) and for the wadding add 1¼ in (3.2 cm).

CUTTING OUT

Make a pattern for the sachets by tracing the template (page 94). For information on tracing templates see page 116. Using the calculated measurements, cut out the following from fabric, interfacing and wadding. Omit the seam/hem allowance on interfacing.
Tissue Box
Top: two fabric, one interfacing
Side: one fabric, one interfacing

line and cut out the centre, ¼ in (6 mm) away from the stitching.

6 Snip towards the stitching and turn right sides out. Roll the seam between fingers and thumbs to the edge, tacking as you proceed. Press well.

7 Apply the lace, with the edge under the opening, overlapping the ends to neaten. Tack in place and edge stitch in position. Trim the outer edges of the top, aligning the ruched edge of the lace with the raw edges of the fabric, making sure there is extra lace at the corners and overlapping the ends to join. Tack and machine stitch. Tack the lace down at each corner, page 112.

8 Turn ¼ in (6 mm) twice along the bottom of the side strip. Tack and machine.

9 With right sides together, pin and tack the side strip to the top, allowing for the joining seam (which is stitched afterwards) to be at a corner; snip the strip as each corner is reached. Starting and finishing 1 in (2.5 cm) from the corner side seam, machine stitch ⅜ in (1 cm) from raw edges. Machine the corner side seam and complete stitching the strip to the top. Remove all tacking.

10 Tack around the top, opening the seam with your fingers underneath. Edge stitch round the outer edge of the top. Trim with a ribbon bow and rose. Remove the tacking.

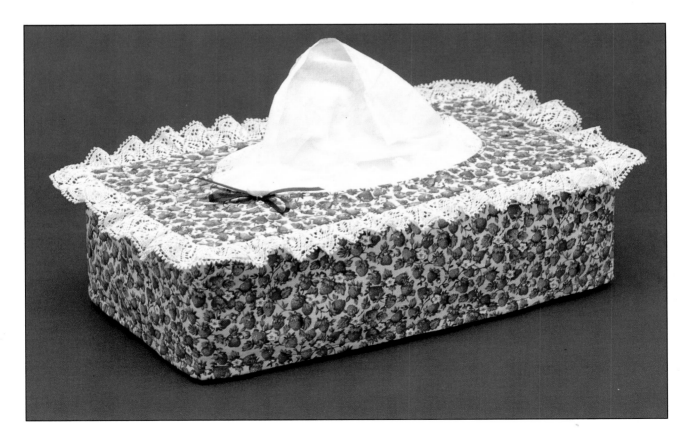

pot-pourri sachets
template

(actual size)

ᵔCOVERED ᵔ HANGERS

Work each process on the two hangers before proceeding to the next step.

1 Mark the centre of the wadding lengthways with a pin and lay the hanger on the wadding with the hook in line with the pin. Pull the wadding up and sew the overlap on top, with large stitches, working from the hook outwards on both sides. Do not pull the thread too tightly.

2 Slip a length of velvet tubing over the hook, secure with a few stitches to the wadding, and neaten the raw edge by tucking in the end and oversewing.

3 Turn $1/2$ in (1.3 cm) to the wrong side of the long edges of the covering strip, and press.

4 Fold in half, right sides together, and curve the ends by drawing around a suitable object with a fabric pen. Machine stitch, trim the seam and turn right sides out.

5 Fold the strip in half and mark the centre with a pin. Place the hanger on the strip, positioning the pin by the hook.

6 Stitch the cover on with small running stitches, starting from the centre and working outwards. Ruche the fabric as you proceed, securing the thread when you have worked around the curves.

POT-POURRI ᵔSACHETS ᵔ

The instructions are for making two sachets at the same time.

1 Turn $1^{1}/2$ in (3.8 cm) at the top on each of the four pieces and press.

2 Trim two pieces with lace, neatening the raw edge at the top and aligning the ruched edge of the lace with the raw edge of the fabric. Tack and machine in place $1/4$ in (6 mm) from the raw edge. Tack the lace down to the right side, page 112.

3 Place one trimmed and one untrimmed piece right sides together. Pin, tack and machine $1/4$ in (6 mm) from the raw edges. Remove the seam tacking.

4 Turn right sides out and remove the tacking, holding the lace down. Fill with pot-pourri. Pleat the top a little way down and stitch to secure.

5 Trim with a ribbon bow and rose, and sew a loop of ribbon on the back.

✧ MORNING TEA TRAY SET ✧

A tray set made to match the bedroom pretties is a most attractive idea.

MATERIALS

- Fabric: 45 in (114 cm) wide, ⅞ yd (80 cm)
- Thin muslin or similar: 18 x 12 in (46 x 30.5 cm)
- Medium thickness wadding: 18 x 12 in (46 x 30.5 cm)
- Thread to match ribbon
- Ribbon: ⅛ in (3 mm), 4½ yds (4.15 m)
- Hook and loop fastener: ⅝ in (15 mm) wide, 8 in (20 cm)

CUTTING OUT

1 For the traycloth, cut one piece of fabric 20 x 15 in (51 x 38 cm); this size is suitable for a tray measuring 17 x 12 in (43 x 30.5 cm).

2 For the napkin, cut one piece of fabric 18 in (46 cm) square.

3 For the tea cosy, first make a pattern following the grid diagram (opposite). Additional information on using grid diagrams is given on page 117. Cut out two pieces of fabric, one of muslin and one of wadding. Trim off ⅜ in (1 cm) from all round the wadding.

TRAYCLOTH & NAPKIN
✧⋮✧

1 Turn ¾ in (2 cm) to the wrong side on the edges, pin and press the fold. Turn ¾ in (2 cm) again and press. Form mitred corners, page 111.

2 Machine stitch the hems and press.

3 To give a decorative finish, sew a ribbon trim on with a zigzag machine stitch, placing it over the stitching of the hem on the right side, and turning it diagonally as each corner is reached. Overlap the ends of the ribbon, turning under the raw edge of the top piece as you complete the trim.

4 Give a final press with a damp piece of muslin and a medium-hot iron.

✧ TEA COSY ✧

1 Lay one piece of fabric right side down, place the wadding on top (there will be a margin of fabric showing all round) and lay the muslin over the wadding.

2 Secure the layers together with a few pins. Turn the work over carefully to have the fabric uppermost and tack, working from the centre outwards. Do not pull the tacking thread tightly.

3 With a large machine stitch, work a freehand design, starting and finishing near the centre. Do not work too much stitching. Pull threads through to the back and knot.

4 Having the right sides together, place the second piece of fabric over the quilted piece. Pin across the centre and in a few other places, then tack the

seam allowance of ³⁄₈ in
(1 cm) all round.

5 Machine stitch, leaving
a gap of 5 in (12.5 cm) in
the centre of one side.
Remove the pins and
tacking. Turn right side out,
slip-stitch the gap to close.

6 Mark a line across the
centre to denote the top
of the tea cosy, tack both
sides of the line and
around the outside ³⁄₈ in
(1 cm) and 1 in (2.5 cm)
from the edge.

7 Mark a line with a
fabric pen ⁵⁄₈ in (1.5 cm)
from the edge for a guide

for sewing the ribbon trim
in place. Apply the trim as
for the traycloth and
napkin, Step 3. Machine
stitch across the centre
between the ribbon lines.

8 Stitch pieces of hook
and loop fastener tape on
the sides, taking the
placement of the handle and
spout from the teapot to
be used into consideration.

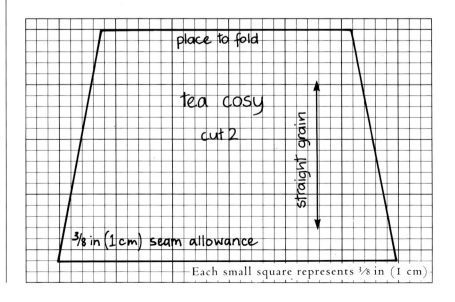

place to fold

tea cosy

cut 2

straight grain

³⁄₈ in (1 cm) seam allowance

Each small square represents ³⁄₈ in (1 cm)

ᴄ᷉ BASKET OF ROSES ᷈ᴗ

A pretty basket of roses which co-ordinates with the bedroom fabric 'specials'.

MATERIALS

- Single satin ribbon, four shades to tone with fabric items: 7/8 in (23 mm) wide, 6½ yds (6 m) total
- Binding wire
- 6 short pine sprigs
- Green ruscus leaves
- Florist's plastic anchor
- Rectangular cane basket with handle: about 7 x 5 x 3 in deep (18 x 12.5 x 7.5 cm deep)
- Florist's plasticine fix
- Dry florist's foam block
- Sea lavender
- 2 pieces of spare bedroom fabric: about 18 x 3½ in (46 x 9 cm)
- Double satin ribbon, contrasting shade: 1/8 in (3 mm) wide, 6 in (15 cm)
- Clear adhesive
- Coloured canary grass

1 Make 21 ribbon roses and six rosebuds on wire stems, pages 115 and 116.

2 Wire the pine sprigs and ruscus.

3 Secure the plastic anchor in the basket base with the plasticine fix.

4 Wedge the foam block firmly on to the anchor so that the top is level with the rim of the basket.

5 Set the pine sprigs in the foam on each side of the handle and pointing outwards from the centre.

6 Fill in with sea lavender, making sure that some overhangs the basket rim.

7 Add the ruscus leaves, distributing them evenly and placing the tallest towards the centre.

8 Fold each piece of fabric lengthwise, with right sides together. Pin and machine stitch with a ¼ in (6 mm) seam, leaving a central gap for turning and removing the pins as you machine. Turn right sides out and slip-stitch the opening to close. Roll the seam between fingers

and thumbs, tack as you proceed and press, using a damp piece of muslin and a medium-hot iron. Fold a single bow from each strip, page 114, securing the centre with the narrow contrasting ribbon.

9 Glue or wire a fabric bow at the base of the handle, either side of the basket.

10 Create a framework of roses by placing one or two of the tallest in the centre as an apex of an imaginary triangle and one or two outwards on either side and nearly parallel with the basket rim, see diagram.

11 Set the remaining roses and buds among the greenery, varying the shades, recessing some of the flowers and remembering that the back of the basket may well be reflected in the dressing-table mirror.

12 Place the canary grass among the roses to soften the outline of the arrangement and to add height and width at the sides.

pine twigs

sea lavender

rose

rose

fabric bow

⤳·STAR OF BETHLEHEM WALL HANGING·⤳

An ideal wall hanging for Christmas which will help to arouse the imagination of young children.

MATERIALS

Use 45 in (114 cm) wide cotton fabric throughout; pre-wash and press before cutting out.

⤳ Fabric – four mix-and-match Christmas designs in the following quantities:
Red dot (fabric 1): ¼ yd (25 cm)
White patterned (fabric 2): ¼ yd (25 cm)
Dark green dot (fabric 3): ¼ yd (25 cm)
Dark green patterned (fabric 4): ½ yd (45 cm)

⤳ Thread to tone

⤳ Lightweight wadding: 18 in (46 cm) square

⤳ Dowelling: ½ in (1.3 cm) diameter, 19 in (48.5 cm)

⤳ Cord: ¼ in (6 mm) diamater, 1 yd (90 cm)

CUTTING OUT

1 Trace the templates (page 102) and cut out in card, accurately adding ¼ in (6 mm) seam allowance on all edges. For information on tracing templates see page 116. Mark the templates A to E as shown.

2 Using the templates, cut out the following shapes in the given fabric and numbers:

Template	Fabric	Number
A	1	16
B	2	16
C	3	4
D	4	8
E	3	8

Borders: cut 4 strips 12½ x 2½ in (32 x 6.3 cm) of fabric 2
Border/corner squares: cut 4 squares 2½ in (6.3 cm) of fabric 1

Binding: cut 4 strips 17½ x 1½ in (44.5 x 3.8 cm) of fabric 3
Hanging loops: cut 1 strip 15 x 3 in (38 x 7.5 cm) of fabric 3

Stitch all seams using the allowance of ¼ in (6 mm) precisely to obtain good results.

1 Following the block diagram (Fig. A), lay out the pieces on a flat surface right side uppermost.

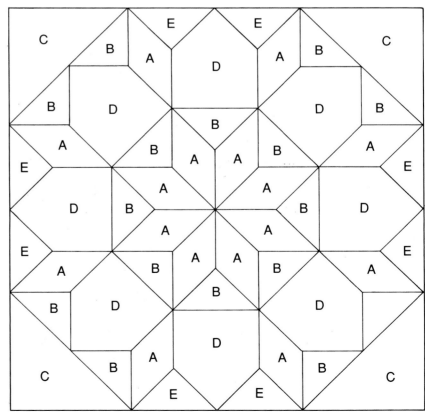

Fig. A

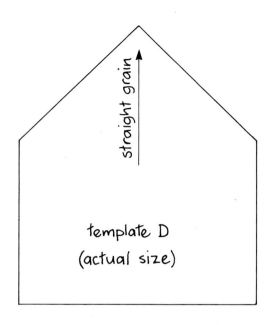

template D
(actual size)

straight grain

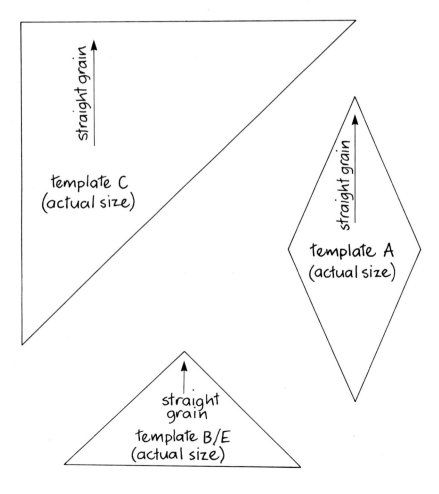

template C
(actual size)

straight grain

template A
(actual size)

straight grain

straight grain

template B/E
(actual size)

2 To assemble the block, stitch the eight A shapes, fabric 1, together. Press the seams open.

3 Stitch the eight B shapes, fabric 2, between the points of the A shapes, starting at the centre point and stitching outwards on both sides (Fig. B). Press the seams open.

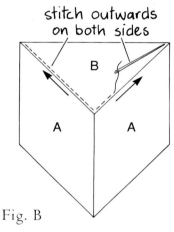

stitch outwards on both sides

B

A   A

Fig. B

4 Stitch the remaining eight A shapes, fabric 1, pieces to the left-hand side of D shape, fabric 4 (Fig. C, opposite). Press the seams open.

5 Stitch D to B all round, then join the edge of A to the adjoining D. Press the seams open.

6 For the corner sections of the block, stitch B shapes between the points of A and D, stitching

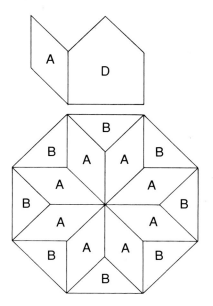

Fig. C

outwards as in Step 3. Press the seams open. Stitch C shapes in place to complete the corner. Press the seams open.

7 To complete the block, stitch E shapes between the points of A and D, stitching outwards as previously. Press the seams open.

8 Place two border pieces to opposite sides of the finished block and stitch with the right sides together. Press the seams open.

9 Stitch a corner square to each end of the two other border strips and stitch in place to complete

the border. Press the seams open.

10 Cut a piece of backing, fabric 4, and wadding about 1 in (2.5 cm) larger than the finished block.

11 Working on a flat surface, lay the backing fabric right side down, then the wadding and the finished block on top right side up. Starting in the centre, baste the three layers together with fairly large stitches.

TO QUILT THE HANGING

1 Either quilt by hand or 'stitch in the ditch', page 111. Quilt sufficiently to achieve the desired effect. Remove basting from the centre.

2 Trim away any excess wadding and backing fabric, ensuring all raw edges are even.

TO MAKE THE HANGING LOOPS

1 Fold the raw edges into the centre lengthways, and press the folds. Fold in half again and tack the pressed folds together. Edge stitch along both sides.

2 Cut the strip into three equal pieces. Fold the strips in half widthways and place them to the back of the work aligning the raw edges, having one in the centre and one at each end placed ¾ in (2 cm) away from the side raw edges (Fig. D, below).

TO BIND THE HANGING

Follow the Log Cabin cloth instructions, page 63.

TO COMPLETE

Bring the hanging loops up and stitch to the binding. Insert the dowel through the loops and tie the cord in position.

Fig. D

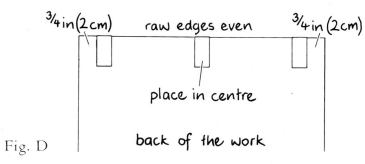

¾ in (2cm)   raw edges even   ¾ in (2cm)

place in centre

back of the work

⌁ CHRISTMAS MOBILE ⌁

With the twisting and turning of the
fabric decorations used for this festive version,
a mobile will keep the little one amused
for quite a while.

MATERIALS

- One panel of fabric tree decorations
- Thread
- Polyester stuffing
- Ribbon
- Square plastic embroidery frame
- Wooden bead
- Adhesive tape
- Glue

1 Cut out the fronts and backs of the decorations, selecting the number required.

2 With the right sides together and matching the partner to each, stitch round ¼ in (6 mm) from the raw edges, leaving the gap marked for stuffing.

3 Snip towards the stitching, taking care not to cut through the stitches. Turn right sides out and stuff. Slip-stitch the gap to close.

4 Stitch a 10–12 in (25.5–30.5 cm) length of ¹⁄₁₆ in (1.5 mm) ribbon or thread to each decoration ready to hang.

HANGING THE MOBILE

1 Tie or glue a 20 in (51 cm) length of ribbon to each corner of the inner section of the frame. Knot the lengths together, about 8 in (20 cm) along the ribbon. Thread a bead on to the ribbons to pull over the knot to neaten, and knot the ribbons together above the bead to make a loop for hanging the mobile.

2 Hang the mobile to position the decorations (a handle or a knob on an open cupboard door could be used). Tie or temporarily fix the decorations with adhesive tape on the corners and sides, keeping the mobile balanced and arranging the decorations at different heights. When all looks right, attach the hanging ribbons permanently with glue and cut off the surplus.

3 Replace the outer section on the frame. Place the mobile in the desired position, making sure it is safe and out of reach of little hands.

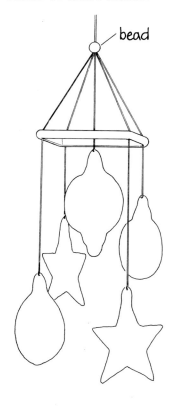
bead

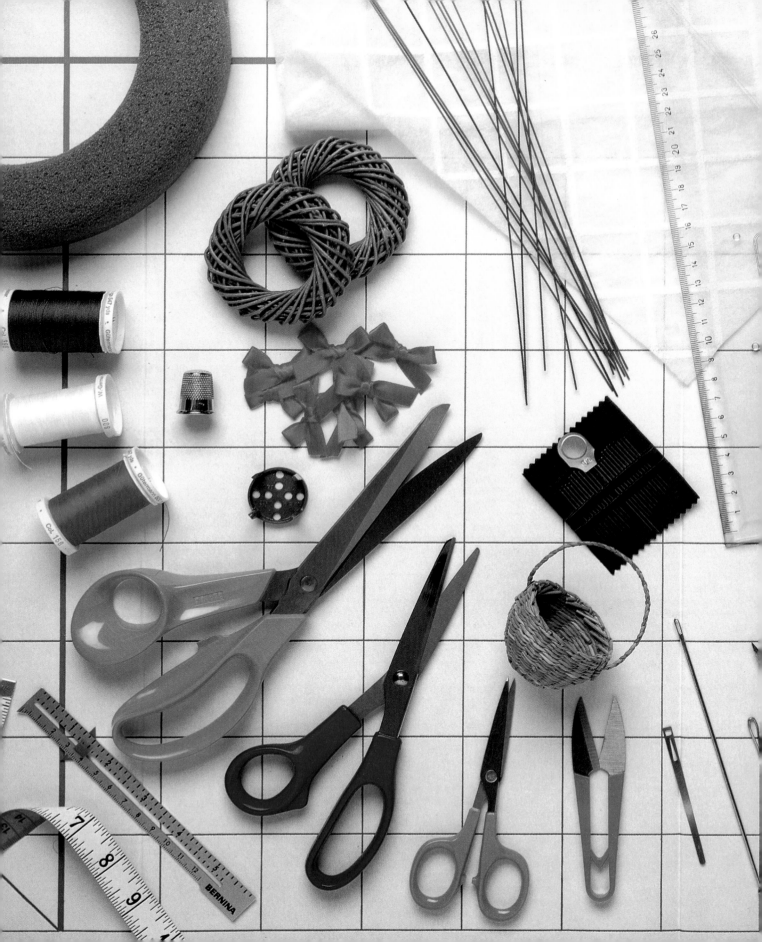

· 7 ·
BASIC
EQUIPMENT
AND
TECHNIQUES

There is a wealth of
information in this
chapter that may prove
helpful when making the
projects whether you are a
beginner or experienced.
Lists of the basic
equipment needed for the
various projects in this
book are provided as a
guide – probably many of
these items will be in the
sewing workbasket or
elsewhere in the home.
The techniques that are
used in several of the
projects are fully explained,
for easy reference.

·

Detailed information is
given on tracing templates,
and on making patterns
from measurements and
from grid diagrams.

EQUIPMENT

SEWING PROJECTS

BODKIN
Round or flat, thick blunt type of needle for threading ribbon into casings.

CUTTING BOARD
A board marked with imperial and metric measurements useful for cutting out and calculating fabric, also for cutting strips when making binding, using the printed bias lines.

FABRIC PENS
Some fade away, others are removed by sponging with water.

HAND-SEWING NEEDLES
An assortment in a house-hold pack gives a choice for most fabrics.

MACHINE NEEDLES
Always purchase the correct 'system' needle for your model of machine (refer to the manual) and have a selection of types and sizes.

PATTERN PAPER
A paper printed with measured squares for grading up diagram patterns.

PINS
Dressmaker's extra fine, long steel pins are most useful.

ROULEAU TURNER
A longer version of a bodkin, the 'eye' can be sewn to the fabric when turning a sewn strip, for example, for ties, through to the right side.

RULER (SMALL)
Preferably a metal one with an adjustable marker.

SCISSORS
Cutting-out: 8 in (20 cm) Should be comfortable to hold. Made from steel, they can be sharpened.
Medium-sized: 6 in (15 cm) For cutting paper only.
Small: For trimming and snipping seams, they should be kept especially for this purpose. For cutting thread, use a pair of thread snips, or an older pair of small scissors.

TACKING COTTON
A soft thread especially made for tacking, it pulls out easily and without harming the fabric.

TAILOR'S CHALK
Made in pencil and tablet form, also a powder which is used in a container with a wheel.

TAPE MEASURE
Made from fibre glass or similar material that will not stretch in use, showing both imperial and metric measurements.

THIMBLE
Usually worn on the middle finger of your sewing hand when hand-sewing.

TRIMMING AND TAPE MAKER
A gadget for making bias strips into binding.

YARD/METRE STICK
Not only useful for measuring but makes marking long lines on fabric or paper much easier.

CARD WORK AND PATCHWORK PROJECTS

CRAFT KNIFE
Select for the purpose 'in hand' as several types are available. It is necessary for the blade to be sharp to cut card precisely.

CUTTING MAT
A special mat to protect tables when using a rotary

cutter, which has a round blade set in a handle. The cutter is designed so that it can be held in either the right or left hand.

PENCILS

2H is ideal for thin lines on card and it does not smudge easily. 2B can be used on the wrong side of fabric to mark seam lines for patchwork.

RULERS

Small to medium lengths, 6–24 in (15–61 cm) are the most useful. A metal ruler is essential when using a craft knife for cutting card.

SEAM WHEEL

A little wheel with a hole in the middle used for marking a 1/4 in (6 mm) seam allowance round templates.

SET SQUARE

Enables the correct angles to be drawn.

GENERAL CRAFT WORK

ADHESIVE TAPES

Narrow plastic tape used for fixing florist's foam blocks to containers, single and double-sided tape used where the fixing must be invisible, and green binding self-adhesive tape, known as 'gutta percha', used to bind wire stems.

ADHESIVES

A hot glue gun is very effective for fixing large cones and heavy items firmly. The tubed varieties, of which there are a large selection, are easier to use for fine work; choose a fairly quick setting one that will dry clear.

CUTTERS

Wire cutters and secateurs, also scissors kept purposely for this work. (Use sewing scissors for cutting ribbons and fabric.)

PINS

A wide range can be used and the choice depends on whether they are to become part of the decoration or are for fixing purposes only. Choose from the following: dressmaker's – for general craft work; lace – very fine, gold in colour, excellent for metallic ribbons; glass-, plastic- and pearl-headed – can be part of the decoration.

WIRE
Obtainable from fine to heavy gauge, but binding wire 28 gauge (0.38 mm) to 32 gauge (0.28 mm) is the most useful.

MISCELLANEOUS

As the following items are used frequently, it is advisable to keep a supply on hand.

COCKTAIL STICKS
For making an anchor for fixing candles to a foam base.

FLORIST'S ANCHORS
Small plastic prongs, often called 'frogs', used to attach florist's foam to a base or container with a fixative such as florist's plasticine. Also useful to enable small light arrangements, such as garland hitches, page 26, to be attached to vertical or horizontal surfaces.

FLORIST'S FOAM
Two main types: one absorbs and retains water, and is intended for use with fresh plant material; the other, which is somewhat coarser, is for use with all dried material.

LACQUER
Clear varnish spray gives a high sheen; hair lacquer is a good substitute, and although it doesn't give a high gloss, it will prevent grasses from shedding seeds.

PAPER BALLS (or similar)
Set on a cocktail stick, covered in glue and rolled in a ground spice, make useful additions of colour to a decoration.

SPICES
Ideal for using when an aroma or colour is required, as well as being effective visually. Whole, seed and powdered spices can be used.

TECHNIQUES

FABRIC TERMINOLOGY

The diagram below of a length of material helps to explain the basic terminology.

PRESSING FABRIC

Pressing is a combination of heat, moisture and pressure. Never underestimate pressing — it is the most important process when sewing to achieve good results. Use a dry iron with a suitable setting for the fabric being pressed and an up-and-down action over a damp piece of muslin.
To press a seam open, first press the stitching in, keeping the layers together as they were for sewing. Open the seam, cover with a damp piece of muslin and press. A light press on the right side, with a dry piece of muslin in place helps to give a professional finish. Where an edge has to be pressed, use the side of the iron with a damp piece of muslin over the work.

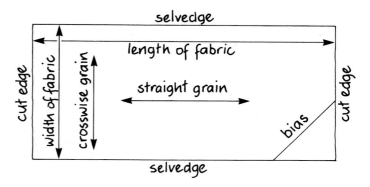

STITCHES

HERRINGBONE STITCH
Worked over the raw edge of a single turn hem. Working from left to right, secure the thread inside the hem with a couple of stitches, and bring the needle up (Fig. A). Take a stitch just above the hem from right to left; moving to the right, take a stitch in the hem from right to left. Continue in this manner, always keeping the needle horizontal to the hem.

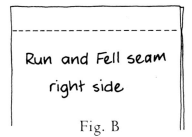

Herringbone stitch

keep needle horizontal to hem
Fig. A

RUN AND FELL SEAM
A strong seam for frequently washed items.

1 Place the two pieces of fabric wrong sides together and machine ⅝ in (1.5 cm) from the raw edges (Fig. B).

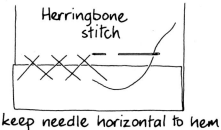

Run and Fell seam
right side

Fig. B

2 Trim away half the seam allowance on one side only (the back of garments). Fig. C.

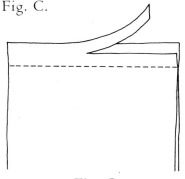

Fig. C

3 With the wider seam allowance on top, press the seam to one side (Fig. D).

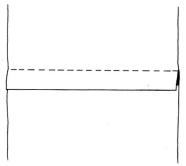

Fig. D

4 Neaten the seam by turning ¼ in (6 mm) and tack down. Machine in place and press (Fig. E).

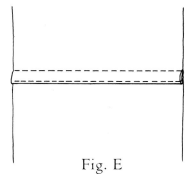

Fig. E

SLIP STITCH
A stitch used to close a gap in an item that has been turned through after machining two pieces of fabric together – for example, the heart and bell Christmas tree decorations and the dining room table setting. Taking small stitches, slide the needle along the fold of the turning, first on one side, then on the other. Pull the thread tight enough to close the gap, but take care not to cause any wrinkles. Press after completing.

STITCH-IN-THE-DITCH
A line of machine stitching worked directly on the line made by the joining of a seam.

TOP STITCH
Machine stitching worked on the right side ¼ in (6 mm) away from the edge. A larger stitch length is generally required.

MITRED CORNERS

The advantage of mitring a corner is that it reduces bulk. Use the hem allowance measurements from the project being made and follow the diagrams and instructions in sequence.

1 Make the first turn of the hem on all sides, and press (Fig. A).

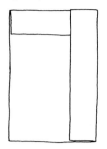

Fig. A

2 Make the second turn all round and press (Fig. B).

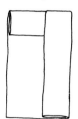

Fig. B

3 Unfold the second turn of the hem, refold on the diagonal, and press (Fig. C).

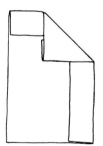

Fig. C

4 Unfold the corner, fold the right sides together and machine stitch along the crease line (Fig. D).

Fig. D

5 Trim the seam to ¼ in (6 mm) and turn the corner right side out (Fig. E).

Fig. E

6 Refold the hem back into position, machine stitch and press (Fig. F).

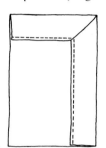

Fig. F

APPLYING LACE

When applying lace as an edging, always allow a little extra for any corners and for overlapping the cut edges. After machine stitching the lace on, tack it down, especially where there is extra fullness, to avoid the lace being caught in the stitching when the back is machined in place.

BIAS STRIPS

Cutting and joining bias strips for piping and binding needs to be done carefully to get a good result. Marking for cutting out is shown in the lay-outs of the relevant items, for example, the toddler's tabard and 'his' and 'hers' aprons. Joining is nearly always necessary to make the strips of sufficient length for items.

The stitching of the strips together, with a ¼ in (6 mm) seam, is on the straight grain.

1 Pin and stitch the seam (Fig. A).

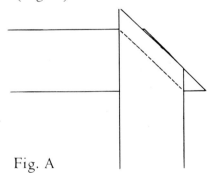

Fig. A

2 Press open and trim off protruding corners (Fig. B).

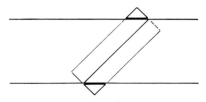

Fig. B

CONTINUOUS STRIP
If a long length of binding is required, it can be made from a rectangular piece of

fabric, which should be twice as long as it is wide. Follow the diagrams opposite in sequence.

1 Cut off a triangular piece of material on the bias from one end (Fig. A).

2 Join, with a ¼ in (6 mm) seam, to the other end (Fig. B).

3 Mark cutting lines for the required width, and at the top and bottom a ¼ in (6 mm) joining seam line (Fig. C).

4 Join top to bottom, to make a tube, right sides together with A meeting B. Machine and press seam open (Fig. D).

5 Cut along the marked lines (Fig. E).

TO MAKE PIPING
Cut the width of the strips to cover the piping and give a ⅝ in (1.5 cm) seam allowance. For jumbo cord used for the hem edge on the floor length cloth, page 22, cut the strips 3 in (7.5 cm) wide.

1 Place the piping cord on the centre on the wrong side of the bias strip.

CONTINUOUS STRIP

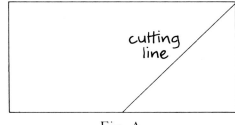

cutting line

Fig. A

¼ in (6mm) seam

Fig. B

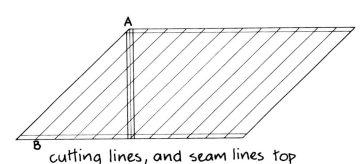

A

B

cutting lines, and seam lines top and bottom, marked on fabric

Fig. C

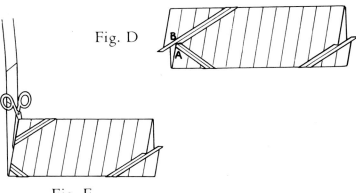

Fig. D

B
A

Fig. E

2 Fold the strip over the cord, and with the raw edges together machine stitch, close to the cord, using a zipper or piping foot on the machine, see diagram.

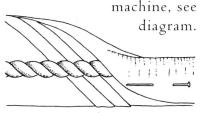

fold strip over cord

TO MAKE BINDING

1 Turn under ⅜ in (1 cm) on each side and press (Fig. A).

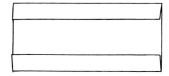

Fig. A

2 Fold binding in half, turned edges together and press (Fig. B).

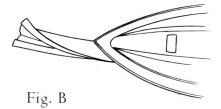

Fig. B

Alternatively, use a trimming and tape marker/ bias tape maker, following the manufacturer's instructions.

TO CURVE FOLDED BINDING

Holding the turned edges, as shown (Fig. C), and pulling gently to make it curve, press with a medium-hot iron.

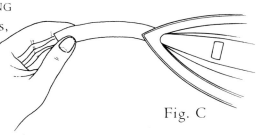

Fig. C

❧ CRAFT WORK ❧

MAKING BOWS

Single bow: fold the ribbon to the desired size, with the loops slightly away from the tails (Fig. A, below). Stitch through the centre or tie with wire or narrow ribbon, which could be of a contrasting colour or texture.

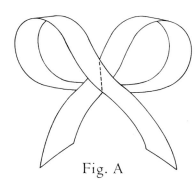

Fig. A

Double or treble bow: fold the ribbon as for a single bow, but repeat the loops twice or three times. Stitch or wire through the centre as for the single bow (Fig. B).

Fig. B

SETTING A CANDLE ON FLORIST'S FOAM

Four cocktail sticks or two hairpins, adhesive-taped to the base of a candle, make an economical

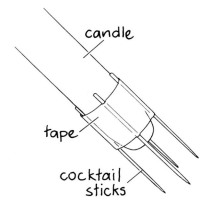

candle

tape

cocktail sticks

and easy alternative to purchasing a candle cup. The protruding sticks or pins are then spiked directly into the florist's foam, see diagram.

CUTTING NAPKIN RINGS AND CANDLE HOLDERS

Cardboard tubes from kitchen paper towels and foil, and toilet paper, can form the base of napkin and candle rings.

1 Lay the tube on a cutting board or wooden surface such as a bread board.

2 Mark the required length from one end, all round the tube, and join the marks with a continuous line.

3 Support the tube with one hand lightly but firmly, and cut along the marked line with a serrated knife or sharp blade, turning the tube into the cutting edge until the two parts are severed.

TO WIRE CONES AND FIX NUTS

Scaled cones, such as pine and spruce, are easily

wired around their lowest circle of scales. The wire ends are then twisted together to form stems. Solid cones, such as cedar and casuarina, are best hot-glued in place. Nuts, such as walnuts, hazels and pecans, can be drilled and wired, but are most easily attached with hot glue.

FISHTAILING RIBBON

A finishing touch particularly suited to plaids and tartans:
1 Fold the ribbon tail in half, edges together. Cut through the two thicknesses from the folded edge to the raw edge at an angle of about 45 degrees.

2 Open out the ribbon to reveal an inverted 'V', or fishtail.

RIBBON ROSES

The diameter of a finished rose is about one and a quarter times the width of the ribbon used, and the length of ribbon required varies with the width too. The following lengths are

a guide for making one rose:
5 in (12.5 cm) of $\frac{1}{4}$ in (6 mm) ribbon
8 in (20 cm) of $\frac{5}{8}$ in (15 mm) ribbon
10 in (25.5 cm) of $\frac{7}{8}$ in (23 mm) ribbon

STITCHED WIRED ROSE

Using single satin ribbon and matching thread, and a rose stub or binding wire to make the stem, follow the instructions.

1 Hold the ribbon with the cut end to the right and the matt side towards you.

2 Bend the end of the length of wire, to a depth equal to the ribbon, and hook it through the upper right-hand corner of the ribbon about $\frac{1}{4}$ in (6 mm) in from the edge (Fig. A). Close the hook to hold the ribbon.

wire hook through ribbon

Fig. A

3 Roll the end of the ribbon inwards from right to left, two or three times, enclosing the wire hook, the wire stem towards you, and stitch (Fig. B).

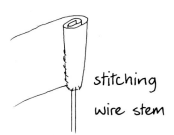

stitching

wire stem

Fig. B

4 Fold the ribbon length away from you, so that the tail hangs downwards (Fig. C).

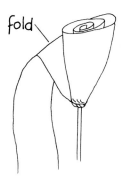

fold

Fig. C

5 Roll the wired end from right to left into the fold, turning tightly at the bottom and loosely at the top, until the ribbon is again horizontal (Fig. D).

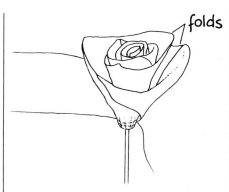

folds

Fig. D

6 Continue folding the ribbon and rolling the rose in this way, stitching at the bottom after each fold is taken up, until the desired shape and size are achieved.

7 To complete the rose, cut the ribbon end off squarely, fold it back and down to the base. Gather the cut edge neatly and stitch to hold. To make just a stitched rose, follow the above instructions omitting the wire.

ROSEBUDS

To make a stitched wired bud, use ribbon as for the rose, plus florist's binding wire and binding tape. Follow the instructions for making a ribbon rose, Steps 1 to 4 inclusive.

1 Roll the wired end over from right to left into the

fold, firmly and evenly, stitching at the bottom.

2 Cut the ribbon off squarely and fold the end back and down to the base. Stitch to hold.

3 Bind the base of the bud and the wire stem with binding tape.

TRACING TEMPLATES

Accuracy is the keyword when tracing templates. Place tracing or grease-proof paper over the page.

1 With a sharp H pencil, trace the shape; using a ruler for the straight lines will help.

2 For patchwork where the template is going to be used many times, cut out the tracing, leaving a margin all round.

3 Stick it to thick card with a suitable glue. Allow to dry completely.

4 Cut out using a sharp craft knife and metal ruler on a suitable cutting surface.

For templates that are for fabric items, cut out on the actual tracing lines and use as a paper pattern.

PATTERNS FROM MEASUREMENTS

Round patterns are easy to make from a piece of paper using the pencil and string method. Tie a piece of string to a pencil, and using the radius of the circle required, measure the distance along the string from the pencil. Secure the string with a drawing-pin in the corner of a folded square piece of paper placed on a suitable surface, and draw an arc.

PATTERNS FROM GRID DIAGRAMS

1 Count the squares on the diagram along the top and down one side.

2 Using pattern paper printed with measured squares, mark the size of paper required and number the lines along the top and down the side.

3 Following the outline on the diagram, put a succession of dots where the shape intersects on a grid line.

4 When the dots have been marked, join them up, first the straight lines using a ruler (or a yard/metre stick if the lines are long), then the curved lines.

5 Write any instructions that will be needed when making the item. Cut out the pattern.

CREDITS

Projects shown on pages 16, 38, 39, 61, 66, 101 were designed and made by Barbara Carpenter.

Projects shown on pages 14, 18, 24, 26, 35, 41, 42, 56, 58, 64, 74, 77, 89, 98 were designed and made by Mary Straka.

Projects shown on pages 22, 23, 30, 32, 36, 41, 45, 46, 48, 53, 64, 69, 71, 78, 81, 84, 85, 88, 92, 95, 96, 104 were designed and made by the Author.

INDEX